Wolfen Wicca

A beginners Journey to Pre-dedication

Author Lady Wolfen Mists

Silver Hoofs & Paws Project

Copyright page
copyrighted ©Nov. 02, 2014
ISBN: 978-0-9790662-4-5

Photo copyrights go to

Image from BigStockPhoto.com

Cover art © by outdoorsman

Page 167, 179, 225, 264, 277, 280, 307, 322

page 49 ©Regi

page 64 © Lynn Earl

page 115 © Micah Keeley

Dedication Page

  This book is dedicated to all those student who over the years have passed through my doors. They inspired me, they challenged me, they made me dig deeper into myself and my beliefs even when I did not want to. They (unknowingly in many cases) guided me, they made my life worthwhile and even in some cases aggravated the crap out of me (no names, you know who you are ☺.) Yet they are all in my heart and I love them deeply for being a brilliant shining beckon in my journey through life. I am so Blessed to have known each of you, thank you for selecting me as your teacher and allowing me to serve.

  It is also dedicated to those out there that really do want to learn Wicca, not just as a hobby but as a true way of life. This book represents over 40 years of my experience on my path of Wolfen Wicca ®. It has been written, rewritten, revised and revised again, over and over. It seems with each new class I taught I added more for not only did I teach my students I was taught, in turn, by them. What a wonderful life experience it has been. I hope you enjoy my life work and if it helps you in anyway that is simply because of the Bright Lady and Lord and not anything I have done, for I simply serve the Light.

Eternal Blessings to you all,
Forever In the Loving Service Of Others
Lady Wolfen Mists

A word on Prededication and Dedication. This books title says it takes you to prededication and that is true, yet those who wish to go further will need to follow the instructions at the end of the book (page 328) and receive a passing grade. It is at this point you will be considered a full Dedicant and will be sent an acknowledgment as such.

Contents page

Be sure to keep your sales receipt or confirmation e-mail of purchase of this book, you will need it later

Human Error		7
Introduction		9
Wolfen Wicca ® Class #1 Cover Page		**13**
Class #1	A general overview of beliefs of Wolfen Wicca	14
Class #1	Short "look" at history	19
Class #1	Who are Pagans and Traditions	26
Class #1	Sabbats	27
Class #1	Mind Training: Basics	32
Class #1	4 count Breathing	35
Class #1	Visualization Red Candle Technique (optional)	38
Class #1	Test What you have Learned	41
Wolfen Wicca ® Class #2 cover page		**45**
Class #2	Ranks or Grades In Wicca	46
Class #2	Goddess Information-Points for all	50
Class #2	Goddess Information- Importance today	52
Class #2	THE Goddess: Importance for men today	54
Class #2	General Points on the God	55
Class #2	Grounding; A basic understanding	57
Class #2	Pathworking: Basics	59
Class #2	Wiccan Rede Breakdown	61
Class #2	Wiccan Rede handout	64
Class #2	Three Fold Law or Law of 3	65
Class #2	Ethics: Lady Wolfen Mists Reprint	67
Class #2	Grounding; Tree Technique Exercise	69
Class #2	Pathworking: Arms of the Goddess (Optional Study)	71
Class #2	Test Yourself	74
Wolfen Wicca ® Class #3 Cover page		**77**
Class #3	Moon Phases and Information	78
Class #3	4 Corner Stones	83

Class #3	Pentagram	85
Class #3	Facts about Chakras	87
Class #3	Chakra Layouts and Points on Body	94
Class #3	Test Yourself and what you have learned	100

Wolfen Wicca ® Class #4 Cover page		**104**
Class #4	Blessing & Curse for your Book	105
Class #4	Book of Shadows and Grimoire	106
Class #4	Magickal Names	108
Class #4	Minor Tools	118
Class #4	Major Tools	121
Class #4	Quick Reference: Qualities of 4 Major Tools	122
Class #4	Record Keeping-List all major tools	125
Class #4	Candle Dressing Handout	136
Class #4	Safe Place	139
Class #4	Path work of safe place *(Optional-Use Kitaro Light of the Spirit here)*	144
Class #4	Test Yourself and what you have learned	148

Wolfen Wicca ® Class #5 Cover page		**152**
Class #5	Things you NEED to know	153
Class #5	Dressing for Circle; what to wear and such	155
Class #5	Pre circle Preparation; Personal Sacred Time	161
Class #5	Incense with charcoal granular, stick or cone	168
Class #5	Circle Casting Directions	172
Class #5	Banishing the circle	180
Class #5	Invoke & Banish Circle Quick reference	185
Class #5	Invoke & Banish Pentagram Quick reference	186
Class #5	Altar Set Up-Wolfen Wicca Style	187
Class #5	Cakes and Wine ritual	188
Class #5	Make Purification Sachet	191
Class #5	Test Yourself and what you have learned	193

Wolfen Wicca ® Class #6	**Cover page**	**195**
Class #6	Spirit Guides (types)	196
Class #6	Summerland	200
Class #6	Soul Sending Rite	203
Class #6	Funeral herbs	209
Class #6	Traditional Sabbat Herbs	211
Class #6	Dangerous Herbs for Pregnant Woman	213
Class #6	Talking Spirit Boards	215
Class #6	Do the soul sending rite and write about it in your Grimoire	217
Class #6	Test Yourself and what you have learned	217
Wolfen Wicca ® Class #7	**Cover page**	**221**
Class #7	Spell to aid in Removing Troubles	222
Class #7	13 goals of a Witch	224
Class #7	Creation Myths	226
Class #7	Meditation: *To see your Spirit Guide*	243
Class #7	Pendulums	246
Class #7	Test Yourself and what you have learned	250
Wolfen Wicca ® Class #8	**Cover page**	**253**

Class #8	Types of Magick;
	    Sympathetic Magick
	    Contagious Magick
		254

Class #8	Power	256
Class #8	Invocation for Law of 3	259
Class #8	Consecration	260
Class #8	Rite of Consecration of Tools	261
Class #8	Dream Pillow Recipe	265
Class #8	Test Yourself and what you have learned	268
Wolfen Wicca ® Class #9	**Cover page**	**271**
Class #9	Psychic Self Defense	272
Class #9	Elements of Magickal Dance	278

Class #9	Sacred Chants	281
Class #9	All in the Perspective	284
Class #9	Healing Ritual	288
Class #9	No Written Test from this point on	

Wolfen Wicca ® Class #10   Cover page — 294

Class #10	Posted Standards	295
Class #10	Key Concepts for Magickal Success	301
Class #10	Dark Night Of the Soul	304
Class #10	Wolfen : Basics Laws to gage a coven by & Other sticky Topics	308
Class #10	Psychic Gifts definitions	314
Class #10	The Cords	316
Class #10	Taking your Measure and pushed into circle	317
Class #10	Covensteads and Covendoms	320
Class #10	Wolf Spirit In Your Daily Life	322
Class #10	Do a Pathwork to find a magickal name	324
Class #10	Write about your Dark Night of the Soul in your Grimoire	325

*******On Becoming Recognized Graduate of this course   328
which results in *PREDEDICATION* Level

Have your purchase receipt ready *********

To; My Students

From: Lady Wolfen Mists

Greetings Student,

Welcome to the new class, I hope you enjoy it as much as I enjoyed putting it together for you. You will notice that throughout the course there may be typos, bad grammar and mis spellings, this isn't because it wasn't checked. It is because it slipped through the editing process and to be frank it's the way I talk. ☺ Yep reading these class are almost like talking directly to me, I was going to change them and make them more professional, more correct with grammar and all, but when I told some of my other students they said don't! That reading the classes was almost like sitting across from me at a table and gave a much cozier feeling than perfection on sterile paper. That my writing (way of talking) to the students was part of the charm of the class and made everyone feel better about themselves. So I kept it the way it is.

I am probably one of the most down to earth people you will ever meet and I don't get really anal (or hung up) about spelling, grammar or typos. I just do my best and expect to make a few writing mistakes, so please forgive any that may appear in advance. The information given in this class is solid and valid and comes from my experiences. Perfect or not in its presentation, it is a work (with sweat, crying, hair pulling and pride) given in love to each of my students. It is my hope that it will help you on your Spiritual Journey. That it is something 20 years from now, you will recall with warmth and love in your heart.

Now with all that said, lets get to the good stuff and open your first class.

Blessings,

Lady Wolfen Mists

Introduction

What Can I say here to introduce this book? It is the result of many years of teaching classes on the tradition known as Wolfen Wicca ®. The book came about at the push of the Goddess to make my courses more available to those seeking and so I have.

Wolfen Wicca® is a tradition I developed, created, manifested and trademarked (that's why the little ® is there). It has been a long process that continues each day as I too continue to learn and put new perspectives, ideas and knowledge into my basket. In Wolfen Wicca I encourage you to use the tradition as a basic guideline to make your own Magick, for you truly are the only one who can know what works for you. I simply guide you, I introduce you to techniques and to practices, I give you basics in the Goddess and God and so on. I help you understand rite and rituals and common items used in the practice of this Religion. Yes I did say religion; **Wolfen Wicca ® is a religion** and not just a bunch of techniques one can apply to be used. It is carved into your heart as the Lord and Lady of Light lead you to your destined space and helps you ascend the spiritual ladder, bringing you ever closer to Their home and heart. I am your minister here, your guide, your helper and I am deeply humbled you have chosen and allowed me to be so.

Also in this beginning page want to make it clear to you that Wolfen Wicca® is **NOT for everyone**. It is NOT the ONLY WAY. For those that are called to it, they are welcome to walk this road beside us. For those it does not fit, they to are welcome to walk with us for awhile, as they look for a path that best suites them and that their truths ring loudest in. All paths are to be respected, none are better than another, none more holy, and none has THE special "in" on the truth. All are our attempts as humans to improve ourselves and to celebrate the divine in all things, including ourselves. So with this in mind we of Wolfen Wicca ® do our best not bash any other religion; we do not make judgments based on such things. We do simply walk our path and hold our truths within our essences as we allow others to discover what it is that works best for them as well. The word respect works best here respect everyone's journey for they are exactly where they are meant to be in this moment in time.

With that said let tell you about the course. This course takes you to Wolfen Wicca® Prededication level as you explore the foundation of what you will be building your spiritual life on. It must

be built strong and firm or it is sure to fail, so if you have any problems be sure to do that section over again until you feel you have it and then move on to the next class.

    These classes were designed to build on themselves so **don't skip around**. Do each class consecutively and things will fall into place for you. Do not place grand expectations on yourself as this will lead to failure, just enjoy what you learn and rejoice in it. If you feel you aren't getting something clearly keep trying, but let it flow as it is meant to and not as you think it should. The universe has a wonderful way of surprising us and giving us what it wants us to have, so be open and go with the flow. No one gets it right off the bat 100% of the time, allow for "delays" and remember there is no failure here because there are no expectations, there is just learning and experiencing and becoming the giant spiritual being you were meant to be.

    For those wanting to go on in their studies to self dedication and 1st degree and have this course count towards that there is a place in the back of the book page_____ that explains how to do that.

OK so let's get to it!

Wolfen Wicca ®
Class #1

© Lady Wolfen Mists Jan.1998

Class #1

Theory

    A brief overview of what is Wicca

    Short "look" at history

    What are Traditions?

    Explanation of Sabbats

    Meditation- Mind Training Basics

    4 count breathing

Practical

    Visualization exercise- Red Candle Technique

    Test check what you have learned

Class #1
A general overview of beliefs of Wolfen Wicca

© Lady Wolfen Mists Jan. 1998

Handout on Wicca

The following is a handout we give to people who are interested in Wicca, some of it is traditional some isn't.. It is by no means the "Last Say" on the subject, but it does give you a general idea of our (our meaning my coven/grove, Sacred Sanctuary: Spirits of Light) approach and what our basic belief systems include. As I said this isn't all inclusive of every Wiccan belief out there, just ours.

What Is WICCA?

By Lady Wolfen Mists © 1991

Wicca is a belief system based in duality. That is to say that we believe in a Goddess and a God. We celebrate living experience through the changing of the seasons. On specific days (called Sabbats) we meet to celebrate the continuing cycle of life, death and rebirth. For example on Lammas (in Aug.) we celebrate our Harvest time. Which is much like "Thanksgiving." We also meet least once a month on the full moon to work and worship our God and Goddess. For example we would ask the Lady and Lord for help in healing someone of an illness or thank the God and Goddess for their help in our lives.

We feel that the Lady and Lord are the embodiment of creative powers found in all things. These creative energies are both positive and negative. Now that's not positive and negative in the sense of good and bad, but in the sense of positive and negative polarities. Yes we are considered a Pagan religion.

On The God and Goddess!

The God and Goddess are both equally important in our religion. Although the Goddess is often times paid "more Attention" to than the God, it is only because He allows this. The Goddess is seen as the Mother Creatress, she who gives us life and nurtures us. Her

power is symbolized in the Moon and the Earth and in all things/animals domestic. We do not worship the Earth or the Moon as many believe we do, we only praise the powerful creative energies that we see in the female energies of the Moon and the earth. We feel, like many Christians, that the Goddess has Three aspects also, these aspects are Virgin, Mother, and Crone, which correspond to the times in a woman's life and the phases of the Moon.

The God is seen very much like the Goddess. He is the provider and the sustainer for us. The God is seen as the Father Creator. His power is symbolized in the Sun and the forests and all things wild, especially those wild animals with horns. Why Horns? In the tribal time hunter's usually hunted things with horns to provide food for the tribes hard dark winter yet to come. An animal with horns was a prime catch as it usually had more meat on it then say a rabbit. So to the tribe the Horns became as sign of abundance and then a sign of divinity, thus the God became seen as one with horns to provide the tribe with food for the coming hard winter. We, as Pagans, do not worship the Sun or the forest but see it as the manifested powers of the God and as such pay homage to such power. Again, like many Christians, we see our God as having three aspects. Theses aspects are Youth, Father, Grandfather and like the Goddess these also correspond with the life cycle of men.

On Satan

Wiccan's don't believe in Satan or any form of Ultimate evil. We feel that all beings make choices in life, some choices are positive in nature adding to the growth of the spirit and adding in spiritual advancement. While other choices are negative in nature, blocking the spiritual evolution of the soul and causing that spirit to have to relearn "the lesson" until they unblock their growth process. So as you can see there is no room for an ultimate evil, as all things must remain in balance and the choices that you make for your own spiritual evolution is 100% up to you.

On Jesus

Wicca doesn't ask you to give up any other beliefs to become a practitioner of this belief system. So if you can incorporate Jesus and Christianity into your own belief system along with Wicca then that's

what works for you. That is YOUR MAGICK and it is just as true as one who doesn't incorporate other religions into their Magick.

My PERSONAL belief on Jesus is this, Yes there was a Jesus, and yes he was a great man. Do I believe he was my personal savior? I guess in a way, yet in the same way I believe that Mohammed and Buddha and many others are. No I do not believe that Jesus was my spiritual savior, but that He was a savior in the sense that he and many others who are leaders in religions. He DIRECTED us to believe in ourselves, showing us that we are all sons & daughters of God & Goddess.

I feel that He shows us that we should love all things and that we must be responsible for our choices in life. Did he die for my sins? No I don't think so. I think he tried to show us what is positive for the soul and what is used as a guide to encourage us to grow spiritually, just as he shows us what is negative and slows the process of growth in the spirit and evolution of the soul.

I feel that many others, not just men, have directed us and guided us to "see" and understand what is positive for the growth of the spirit and what causes blocks. Once this has been shown to you, you are the one who makes conscious decisions as to what you choose to do with your life what lessons you will learn and what you will not. Up until that point you were still making those choices but not on the conscious level, on the subconscious level.

What's this About Lessons?

We believe before you incarnate into this physical plane, Earth, you contract with the God/dess on what lessons you would wish to learn in this life. Perhaps in this life you must learn compassion, and you choose to do this through the use of pain and illness. Perhaps you will learn happiness this time around so that you have a balance (there's that word again) from which to draw from on your spiritual growth and evolution. In all lives there are many lessons we choose to learn, if we accomplish learning this lesson then there is no need to repeat it, but if you fail to learn the lesson that you contracted for then you must return to learn it until you get it right. This also accounts for the cycles in your life, those situations that always seen to occur over and over again.

What About That Star That You Wear?

The Pentagram is one of the most misunderstood symbols that we have. To followers of the Craft, it is one of our most Holy Signs of Protection, sort of like the Christian Cross or the Jewish Star of David.

OK I understand that but what does it mean? The Pentagram denotes all the elements of creation and the spirit of man, how they interact and are interdependent on each other. The top point of the star is mans spirit, the following right point is water, then fire then earth then air, coming back to Mans spirit. The circle that surrounds the star is the symbol of birth, life, and death and rebirth.

What does it mean when the star is inverted? This is the part that has really gotten a bad rap. Satanists, and modern media as well as a few others that could be named here have taken this symbol and made it represent Satan. Yet to followers of the Craft all that an inverted Pentagram means is, coming from the spiritual plane to the material plane and brings those attributes with you. That 's it, see nothing to do with Satan. You may see another type of Pentagram; it shows a Pentagram right side up with a smaller one inside inverted. To followers of the Craft this means, As it is above, on the spiritual plane, so be it below, on the physical plane. See it's not so scary once you really get the facts.

What about Sacrifices?

The Craft is a very gentle religion and we do not believe in letting blood or killing any thing. We do not sacrifice animals or people or any thing of that nature, as movies often show. The closest thing to a sacrifice one might find in a Grove, is that of food or libations, maybe flowers or something along those lines. When the food and libations are set out, it is with the full knowledge that animals may partake of them and thus, the never ending cycle of life, death, and rebirth is continued.

Do You Have Any Rules You Live By?

Wicca is a very open religion that encourages personal growth in all areas. Someone once said trying to make Wiccans follow rules is sorta like trying to herd cats, it just ain't done. Thats how it is with rules. We have no "Thou Shall Not's" that are set down by our

Goddess and God. Our religion has no set doctrine or dogma really. It is for this reason that if you go to 100 different Groves/Covens you may find 100 different ways of doing things. However we do all have one thing we agree upon, in some make or manner, and that is called the WICCAN REDE which is thoroughly covered in class #2. Basically says "Do what ya want so long as you Hurt No One" So that is a short overall of what we are and what we believe. I hope I have managed to show you that we are not evil and do not serve Satan or any other "evil" being.

Remember Tolerance is a two sided coin, what you give is what you receive.

BLESSED BE,
Lady Wolfen Mists

Class #1

Short "look" at history

© Lady Wolfen Mists Jan.1998

A Very Quick Historical Overview

I wont dwell a long time on this as there have been entire books written on the History of Wicca, many of which are much more scholarly than what I could write. But it never hurts to have a general background of where you're coming from and that's what I would like to try and provide for you a general back ground.

Wicca is a Shamanisitc Nature religion, that's been around in one form or another since the dawn of time. It involves a worship of both a God and Goddess. It is called paganism, which in Latin means "country dweller." We are called, by the mainstream Christian religion, a "Heathen Religion." Yet when one looks at the words, heathen merely means "one who lives on the heaths" in opposition to one who is rich and lived inside the castle areas of days long gone by. Thus Wicca turns out to be a religion for the common ordinary people!

But what does Wicca mean?

Many different scholars see the root word Wicca coming from many different places. For our purposes here we will refer to it in the Old Saxon usage, meaning "Craft of the Wise." Other definitions include "to bend" or 'to change in accordance with ones desires." Some times you will just hear it called "The Craft" The female practitioners of Wicca are called Wicce (pronounced Wick-key) The male practitioner are referred to as Wicca (pronounced Wic-ka). Just as a side note Wicca is often called a Goddess religion. As such, I find a certain level of irony that a Goddess based religion is generally identified by society as, Wicca (the name for its male practitioners)

Tribal Times

During the tribal days, when people lived in caves and off the land, the religion ran strongly. The ties to the Goddess and God were many. The religion was used to explain the many different forces of nature to these peoples. Insuring they could have a better understanding of what was going on around them and so that they

could interact the spiritual levels through such knowledge. Roles for the Goddess and God grew each taking on aspects of importance to the tribe and its members.

It was at these tribal times that the Goddess was first seen as the life bringer and greatly revered and praised when the tribe increased. Increasing the tribe was no small matter as it insured safety, workers, and power of those members already with in the tribe. The Goddess was also seen in the aspect of cleanser and healer of the sick. Another not so small matter to the tribe, as all members needed to stay strong and healthy to everyone's benefit within the tribe. Fertility on all levels was a role accorded to the Goddess and in spring and summer she was seen as abundant and in full blessed bloom.

The God aspect of life was not over looked either, as the tribe saw Him as the Great Hunter who fed and sustained the tribe in the cold and lean winter months. He helped them to prosper in the material sense and He was the Father defender of the tribe against any and all enemies.

Thus the balance was struck in harmony with all things and in the minds of the people. The Female/yin energies and the Male/yang energies flowed over the world. The world grew and prospered, the tribes grew, and soon became settlement, then towns, then kingdoms, and many different religions evolved and spread. With this growth and movement came new ideas of religion.

The results of Christianity on Wicca

The dualistic balance of the Goddess and God that had worked for the common people for so long was removed, and in its place was a religion of only One God. This God was male and thus a male dominated view of religion now swept over the world. A religion that pushed, dominated, coerced, and even killed those who refused to accept it or change their beliefs.

Men were now seen as superior to women, instead of side by side. Women once seen as Life Giver and Healer, was now unclean and impure. The root of all evil. The one who caused humanity to be forced for perfection and the Garden of Eden?

Sex and the continuous cycle of life, revered for its important significance, to the tribe, was no longer seen as a normal sacred act, to be enjoyed and blessed. It was now views as a sin and only to be tolerated as an act of procreation.

The God figure, who once sat hand and hand by the side of the Divine Mother, was now relegated to a servant of Satan or even the devil himself. All of this was quite a change for the people and unrest and secret religious groups abounded. The Church couldn't have this as it threatened their power and as such the next step developed....

Healers Outlawed

It should be noted that at this time women healers were outlawed. Only doctors were legal and allowed and since women couldn't attend college the profession that so many women once practiced with much honor was not stripped from them and made illegal. Women who still practiced healing's and mid wifery were doing so outside the law and risked death or imprisonment, and were considered "poisoner's."

This was the male attempt to keep women "in their places." It mainly affected those women who used this as their only income, this was usually women with little or not financial help and who were widows or never married and lived alone, with no family to help in their care as they aged.

Since Doctors usually were expensive (look at today's doctors prices) or didn't live in the smaller burgs and town it was often hard to get the medical attention needed when something happened. So the towns people continued to use the Healers and Mid Wives, often in secret and in fear. Most officials in these small out of the way places turned a deaf ear to this, as they also used them and nothing much was done. That is until a "Witch Finder" (a person from the church whose job it was to seek out evil witches) came to town and began a frenzied hunt. It should also be noted that the church paid these witch finders for every witch they found, so it would be smart to keep finding the evil ones if you wanted to get paid. Think about it...

The Burning Times

Then came the "Burning Times," also called "The Woman's Holocaust". I will not go into the numbers of the many who were

condemned to Death, as there is much argument over this by the scholars. Some say as many as 9 million, other say much less. We have enough proof in names/sex and places to say definitely over 300 thousand. History shows us many record's were lost or burnt or just not recorded properly. There are entire towns (especially in France) where these Witch-hunts went on so long that only 3-4 people survived untainted or unaccused. I personally believe the numbers to be higher than 300 thousand, in the 9 million range. Yet numbers are not really the point here. Be it 1 or millions I say even 1 death due to religious belief is 1 to many. The Burning times are usually considered to cover the early 1200's to the very late 1500's or early 1600's. The persecutions themselves were seen as a big business draw and an ideal moneymaker for the town. The cost of the trial was charged to the victim's estate or the victim's town/shire. Many people came from all around to see the trials and the deaths that resulted from these circus trials. There was much "selling" of goods on these days, in the cities and towns these trials were performed in.

Imagine this if you will, you're a business man things are not going well for you. No one is coming into town to buy much you've got to get their attention, something to draw them in...but what? A witch trial!

So someone is accused of witchcraft, everyone from all over not wanting to miss anything flock to the towns where the trial is being held. There are seller's stands set everywhere and people come like it's a fair. You make tons of money and the trial is charged to the victim's estate. What a deal!

Now I'm not saying that it was that way for every victim, but more often than not the trials brought financial relief to the towns business and as such who was gonna stop it.

The trials even became a place for social gatherings, when they weren't accusing actual people in England may people would gather on weekends and burn cats (especially the black ones.) The belief was that cats were the familiars of Witches and as such were demons or witches who were incarnated into cats bodies and waiting to return to a physical human body. In any cases cats were evil!

The people would gather and start a bonfire at a crossroads that had 4 intersections, and put a bunch of cats in a basket. Then they would light the bonfire and hang the cats over the fire until they burnt to death. Shouting such things as "demons be gone" and

"Witch demons, die!" The cats screaming and yowling could be heard for miles, in fact the more they yowled the happier the watchers became saying that the demon was being painfully sent back to hell. The participants would bring their entire families, including the kids, to watch this gruesome sport and often held a picnic at the site. They made an entire fun day of the event.

Now I don't know about you but watching or listening to a cat burn to death is not a loving or fun thing to do, and I wonder at this point in history if the demons weren't outside the baskets holding torches! How cruel and sick, and all done in the name of a God who loves us all, every creature great and small!

These were sad times and a stain on humanity yet we don't often see much attention given to it historically, but this is because the victors write the events and what society is gonna tell their hidden shameful secrets. No it is not something the great Christian Church would want to discuss in this day and

age. Now don't get me wrong I do not blame this on the teachings of Jesus or all of Christianity, I see this as purely a political, financial and social movement created by mankind.

And what do I base that on? Well we see more women than men in the trials, that's not to say there weren't as many men practitioners as women, but due to the society at this time Women had little access to money and couldn't buy their way out as easily as men. Also the women and men who were usually charged with these types of crimes were peasants, widows and single women who often worked (illegally by the way) as healers and mid-wives.

To me this is indicative of the continuous subjugation of a class (in this case women) with blatant political vying, and open economic gain, by subjugation of said class. In two words the burning times was about POWER and CONTROL!

So In Conclusion

As I said in the beginning this is by no means an in-depth look at the burning times its just meant to give you something to draw from. There are many fine books out there that discuss the burning times and the history and development of Witch Craft (Wicca) in a much better way than what my limited knowledge can give. If you're

interested I encourage you to check it out. Its important to know your history where you came from and what those before you suffered so that you can be where you are today.

Here are a few of my last thoughts on the subject. Although the "burning times" are said to be legally over in this country (in other countries, like Africa, they are still killing and stoning and burning women who are called witches) we still live in fear. Many fear for the loss of a job if their faith is found out, others fear the loss of child because an ex may take the "devil worshiper" to court. Others fear loss and being ostracized from friends and family if someone finds out. Sure its now illegal to fire you on basis of religion but it does happen (sometimes wrapped in other reasons) and we all know it. They don't press, stone or burn us in this country any longer, now they fire, starve, disown, and (in some cases) lock us in mental health facilities. Hey we have come a long way haven't we?

How can we fight this mentality, how can we explain what we believe? How can we stop the fear that drives them to hurt us? Through education and honesty. By living a life that others would aspire to. By having tolerance, compassion, honor, and wisdom. These are the things that fight ignorance and the tools we must use.

Forgiveness doesn't mean the person doesn't have to repay for what they did (karma will see to that) forgiveness means we understand and accept and hope all grow from the painful experience. So when you open the broom closet you have had shut for so long, an inch at a time, remember education, tolerance, compassion, honesty and wisdom these are all stored within you and are ready for the sharing.

One more thought that I hear from many Witches, (especially new ones who have just found their path) is the automatic hate of Christianity and all things Christian. The actual teaching of Jesus are very pagan/wiccan/metaphysical and fit very nicely into our belief system. It is the teaching of the "Church" that causes problems and does not easily fit into our belief system. So it's not the words of Jesus that hurts us but the word (doctrine) of men in the church that hurts us, but what else is new.

Sure there are those Christians out there that yank your chain and call you names and tell you your going to hell. Understand that they have just as much a right to their religious belief's as you do. Don't get into arguments with them, and NEVER NEVER waste your

time arguing their Bible with them (however tempting it maybe, been there, I know how it is.) Explain to them that you will never see eye to eye on this and if they want to discuss it in a learning way your open to sharing, if they want to condemn and become adversarial with you thank them for their interest and move on. They will, by their own actions (and I've seen this over and over) look like a total fool. If you attempt to "engage" with them you risk the same happening to you, and anything you have earned (respect wise from others) is in jeopardy of falling apart.

Remember always Tolerance is a two-sided coin**, to get it we must give it!** No matter if we agree to what the other person is saying or not, **We must practice tolerance**. Believe me it will be hard but once you start, besides having a much shorter tongue from biting it so often, you will begin a wonderful habit of not speaking before you think.

Pick your battles wisely, remember what you do, and how you present yourself to others is how they will think of all pagans. If you make a mistake admit it move forward but do your best to live a good full life with respect to yourself, the Goddess and God and others. You have chosen an old and worn path, many have walked before you and fought hard to be accepted and to share, don't let them down and don't Let the Mother & Father down. Be Open, Loving, Forgiving of other blunders (there will be many from inane questions to do you kill babies and animals, to do you really wear those Halloween witch hats?) and Understanding. Show kindness at every chance, give dignity to all and respect to everything in creation for all is Sacred, and ask yourself when in doubt if this is how the Goddess and God would want others to see them. Then act on the answers inside your head, you are Their Child and you really do know the way home and what is expected of you. So Bright Blessing on your journey and may you bring only the best into your life and the lives of all you touch.

Class #1
Who are Pagans and Traditions

© Lady Wolfen Mists Jan.1998

What exactly are Pagans;

Pagans are viewed as just about any religious group that is outside the acceptance of mainstream Christianity. They would include such "heathen" belief systems as Jews, Hindus, Islam, Druids, and Wicca, just to name a few. There are many many pagan sects, but not all pagans are Wiccans. So when someone says, "I'm pagan," don't automatically think that that means they are Wiccan. It simply means their faith falls outside the mainstream Christian religion of what is acceptable.

So remember **all Wiccans are pagans but not all pagans are Wiccans,** got it?

Traditions, What are they

You are at a gathering and someone turns to you and says "What Tradition are you?" You panic, what do they mean What tradition? You're a Wiccan, a witch (if you like.) What more is there? Ton's more. In Wicca (like in Christianity) there are different sects that one can follow (much like denominations in Christianity.)

Right now you are learning **Wolfen Wicca®, founded by Lady Wolfen Mists in 1982**. So your tradition would be Wolfen Wicca ®. Yet someone else may follow a different tradition like Eclectic, Gardenarian, Faery, Alexandrine, Egyptian or Celtic or many many other types.

Each has its own way of doing things, each has its own Pantheon of Gods and Goddess they call on. Each is special in its own way and just as valid as the next. None is really any better than the other (bet you thought I'd say Wolfen Wicca was best didn't you, I think it is for me but it may not be so for others.) Most all traditions work at improving the self and coming into the Higher Self and Honoring the Lady and Lord. The sacredness of creation, the changing of the seasons and the ability to work as you will as long as it harms no one else.

So when someone asks what tradition you are, they are merely wanting to know what group and style you follow to worship.

In another class (a 200 class) you will be given a list of traditions and what they follow and who founded them, but for right now this is enough for you to know.

Class #1
Sabbats

© Lady Wolfen Mists Jan.1998

THE SABBATS

The Sabbats are those times of the year when we (as witches and others in nature religions) celebrate the Great Circle of Life, as it has been acted, and reenacted out in the changing of the seasons and in the renewal of the Earth around/through us.

There are 8 basic Sabbats a year or "Days of Power'. These holidays fall into one of two main categories. The first category being the Major or Fire Festivals which contain:

IMBOLG

BELTAINE

LUGHNASADH (pronounced lewg-naw-sod)

SAMHAIN (pronounced so-wen)

The second category is the Minor or Lunar festivals which contain:

SPRING/VERNAL EQUINOX

SUMMER SOLSTICE

AUTUMN EQUINOX

WINTER SOLSTICE

At each festival (Sabbat) either the God or Goddess is said to rule that time of the year, and as such that gender (the Lady or Lord) is highly honored in the festival itself. Many thanks and reverence is given to the Goddess and God and the celebration is a joyful one with a good time for everyone involved. Usually no real work is done on a Sabbat; work is usually saved for the monthly Esbats (full moons). Yet there have been exceptions to this rule, like say there was an emergency (example a healing was needed) or if the spell or magick could only be done on this specific day. In general however, Sabbats are times of thankfulness, great joy, humble reverence, and fun. They are usually very inspirational and touch each member in a special way that is known only to them.

The following contains the common names and general descriptions of what is celebrated at that particular Sabbat. The dates are general dates that the Sabbats are celebrated on, and really depend on where you live in the world; these dates reflect North American dates. You will notice that I have started with Samhain, the Witches New Year and went from there.

Samhain Sabbat - (Hollowe'en) Oct. 31

At this time we celebrate the "death" of the God and bid him farewell. The Holly Lord waits to take his place, yet we know that the God isn't forever wrapped in a cloak of darkness but will return and be reborn at Yule.

It is at this time that we honor those who have crossed over, and often set a feast to our ancestors. Here the veils that part the worlds of spirit and physical reality are at the thinnest and can be most easily crossed.

Winter Solstice - (Yule) Dec. 21

At this time we celebrate the rebirth of the Lord to the Bright Lady. It is on this night that it is the shortest day of the year and the gift of renewal of the sun (son) is given to us as a promise of the wonder of re-birth of spring that is still yet to come.

In celebration of the return of the Sun (son) many Wiccans burn a candle in the window to honor this rebirth, and to guide the magick of "life" to their homes. The Goddess takes time to renew herself from the labor she has gone through and all rejoice at the new life that has been given to us once again. Here we recognize that from death comes rebirth as shown in this Great wheel of the Year.

Imbolg- (Imbolc, Candlemas) Sabbat - Feb. 2
(Also know as Lady Wolfen Mists birthday, that me, just in case ya wanted to know hee hee)

At this time we celebrate the "quickening" and the physical renewal of life under the snows of winter. Winter has been long and cold and plants and colors begin to germinate in the ground. Spring is well within sight as the Wheel of the year slowly turns.

Imbolg was also called the festival of lights, traditionally many pagans would light bonfires or wear crowns with candles in them to "lure the suns return" and to speed up the return of spring.

You will see many self-dedications and Initiations happening at this time of the year as this is also known as the sabbat of purification. The Gods power begins to grow as the earliest signs of spring creep forward.

Ostara- (Spring/Vernal Equinox)- March 20

At this time we celebrate the first day of our return to spring, as light begins to over take the darkness. Fertility runs in abundance here and the light definitely returns, the days are growing longer as the nights get shorter. The Virgin Goddess gives blessings and fertility and abundance freely at this time. All things are renewed, fresh, and growing.

This is a wonderful time of new beginnings, the planting of life with seeds, time for action that has been stored from the long winter.

Beltane Sabbat - May 1

At this time we celebrate the young Lord and Lady moving into maturity, sexuality runs strong at this time. The young Lord grows into manhood and the young virgin Goddess becomes a Woman. Love abounds in the air at this time. It is at this time the Goddess becomes pregnant with the child that will be born at Yule. The world enjoys the traditional "Lusty month of May" and the fertility of the world is celebrated.

Today's pagans celebrate the fertility and abundance in a ritual that centers on this subject, but caution members to be discriminating when celebrating sex with another. With all the diseases around today one can ever be too careful! Also the sharing of the body/soul should be done between persons that are already involved, and not with total strangers. Giving yourself to another is a sacred act and should be undertaken in a sacred manner.

At this time one should wrap themselves in love and decorate the home in flowers and bright colors. At Beltane we see the return of vitality, of passion and hopes attained.

Summer Solstice -(Midsummer's or Lilith)- June 21

At this time we celebrate the powers of nature that have reached their highest point. The Lord is as powerful as He will become and from this point on, both he and the Lady begin to move towards old age. It is at this point that He is at his peak of power after this day His strength begins to diminish. But for now the world is running abundantly with magick and fertility. This is a great time for just about any magick you would want to do, love purification, fertility, health, protection from the winter to come.

Lughnasadh- (Lammas)- Aug. 1

At this time we celebrate the very first harvest of the seeds we have put into the abundant earth. They have grown and are harvested for the coming winter months when food will be scarce. Traditionally the first corn is taken and baked into a loaf and offered to the Bright Lady and Lord in thanksgiving for the bounty that is yet to come. The Gods power is failing here as the nights begin to grow longer and youthful strength fails.

Autumn Equinox - (Mabon) Sept. 22

At this time we celebrate the last of the harvest that was begun at Lughnasadh (Lammas). We are now ready for the onset of winter and the long darkness that is ready to descend upon us once more. The Gods power has declined and he tires easily. Now is the time to finish up unfinished business.

Here day and night are equal and the God prepares for his inevitable journey, once more, to the underworld. The Goddess knows what is to come and she silently morns the loss of her love, yet she takes refuge in knowing that as the cycle of life continues, and as the power wanes, a bright new born son (sun) will be reborn at Yule. And the Wheel turns once more!

Sabbat chart

Sabbat Name	Southern Hemisphere Down Under	Northern Hemisphere *USA, Canada & such
Winter Solstice (Yule)	20-23 June	20-23 December
Candlemas (Imbolc, Imblog)	1st August	2nd February
Vernal Equinox (Ostara)	20-23 September	20-23 March
Beltaine (Beltane)	31st October	1st May
Summer Solstice (Midsummers)	20-23-December	2-23 June
Lammas (Lughnasadh)	2nd February	1st August
Autumnal Equinox (Mabon)	20-23 March	20-23 September
Samhain (pronounced so-wen)	1st May	31st October

Class #1
Mind Training: Basics

© Lady Wolfen Mists Jan.1998

Mind Training: Meditation-Questions answered here

1. What is Meditation?
2. Why we Meditate?
3. What clearing (quiet) your mind really means

1. What is Meditation?

Meditation is training your mind so that such power can be focused in such a way as to improve the physical, emotional & spiritual essences of yourself and the environment around you. Webster New World Dictionary defines meditation in the following manner;

Deep continued thought or solemn reflection on sacred matters as a devotional act.

As true as the above may be meditation is this and so much more. For the magickal practitioner, meditation is the strong foundational floor you must have before you can go any further. When doing meditation one often finds the visualization is the next step. This is mandatory in any successful spellcasting so you can see how important meditation (or mind training) really is. You can study all the books and techniques you can find on magick and if you fail to properly train your mind (not be able to meditate) you wont ever really be able to grasp all that could have been available to you.

2. Why We Meditate?

First off meditation prepares the mind for the next step of release of the spirit to higher Astral/Etheric levels. Yet there are many other reasons for meditation also. Here are just a few;

On the Physical Level

To alleviate stress, lower blood pressure. Reduce daily tension; reverse the effects of aging.

On the Mental (mind) Level:

To stop or eliminate undesirable behavior, To increase creativity and intelligence levels, to open new perceptions to life, to improve focus and concentration of mind- body oneness.

On the Spiritual Level:

To connect with the "SOURCE." To connect with Higher Self. To learn the inter-connectives of all things in the universe and where we fit in. To learn how to focus and concentrate spiritual energies into positive thought forms and see them manifest in the physical realm. To soothe the soul, renew the spirit and re-energize the convictions of your own personal Spiritual Quest.

3. What clearing your mind really means

Most people believe that when they meditate they must clean everything from their mind until it is this big blank state. Nothing could be further from the truth; in fact the act of forcing yourself not to think makes it impossible to have a clear mind, because you are **thinking** about it all the time.

No the mind just isn't set up to work in such a way. When you meditate you learn to quiet your mind and focus on specific thoughts. As other thoughts and images creep in, and they always do at first, you gently dismiss them and re-direct your thoughts back to the central idea. This is where the words focus and concentration come in. For example you are trying to meditate on reaching the Goddess. You sit quietly, maybe play your selected music, begin your deep breathing (see class #1 section 4 count breathing for exact procedure) and feel yourself focusing on going there. You are seeing in your minds eye space and stars, you feel yourself moving. You go through the darkness of space and feel yourself in a deep green meadow; your mind is focused and pure. You can even smell the flowers, then………
a list of groceries you need to pick up pops up in your mind: Milk,

Cookies, Bread, and so on. Just take a deep breath acknowledge the list and then gently dismiss it, refocus your attention on the thoughts of flowers and the Goddess.

As you work at the meditation and concentration you will find the images get more vibrant. The feelings, smell, taste; all of it is more "real." The time length that you can hold your meditative mind on a specific thought will lengthen, as you learn to visualize and focus and concentrate. So don't be disappointed by intrusive thoughts at first it's all part of the normal process of growing.

Class #1
4 count Breathing

© Lady Wolfen Mists Jan. 1998

4 count Breathing Technique

Breathing is a useful tool, we all do it! It keeps us alive; feeling the flow of oxygen into our body gives us precious life giving energy. What would we do without it? It is this energy, which we often take for granted that we need to direct our attention to. By learning to control the flow of energy that streams through us we can learn to enter trance like states that allow us access to various astral planes.

One of the easiest breathing techniques is 4-count breathing. It allows for control and focus as well as body relaxation. With this technique I would like for you to "visualize or know or feel," what ever one works best for you, that you are taking in pure clean positive life essence as you breath in (inhale in through your nose). Then when you exhale, or breathe out do so through your mouth. While doing this visualize or know or feel that these escaping energies are full of all the negative, mis aligned energies in your body. That's where the focus of your mind should be, in the beginning anyway, at least until you get completely comfortable with it.

Now here is the step by step procedure, remember to visualize, as this is a needed key to success.

1. Find a comfortable place to relax. Beginners may want to sit up in a chair, arms on arm rest or at sides, feet flat on the store. This will help you to not fall asleep, a common problem for beginners.

2. Remove any restrictive clothing or jewelry (watches, rings.) make sure the phone is off the hook or cant be heard where you are. There's nothing worse then almost getting there to be interrupted by some person asking you if you are happy with your phone company. An added point, I like to make sure there's

a glass of water close by and tissues, in case I start to cough just to be safe.

3. Close your eyes and begin to breathe in through your nose. Visualize pure positive energies entering your body.

    Inhaling to the count of 1...2...3...4...

    Feeling the air filling your lungs all the way up to 4.

4. Now hold that breath as you count

    1...holding 2 holding   3... 4...

5. On 4 begin to exhale through your mouth, seeing all the negative mis aligned energies leaving your body. Exhaling all the while to the count

    1...2...3....4....

6. Now hold with the air exhaled to four count again

    1...2...3...4...

7. Begin the inhale count again, fully expanding the lungs while you count

    1...2...3...4...

Continue this cycle for about 5-10 minutes. Beginners should try for as long as comfortable and work up. Pay attention to how the body feels/relaxes. Pay attention to the rhythm of breathing process and how the heart interacts with this technique. Do this a few times until you feel comfortable enough to do it without getting caught up in the steps you know that feeling of am I where I'm supposed to be is this #2 or #4. Am I on hold or inhale, that's getting caught up in the numbers.

      The next step once you get the 4 count breathing down is a visualization exercise. Now not everyone can visualize in their minds as well as others. Some can actually "see" what they are trying to visualize, others just "know it" or sense it there, some "feel it," "hear it." While there are others who "taste it." All of those are equally valid ways of visualization in the minds eye. So whatever comes most natural to you is acceptable.

This class is optional for those who want to learn more "hands on" applications

Class #1
Visualization Red Candle Technique (optional)

© Lady Wolfen Mists Jan.1998

Items you need to have to do this practical section

1 red candle

1 candle holder

Matches

Special Notebook just to record practical work in from this course

Red Candle Technique

So now you have 4-count breathing down we can move on. This section covers the next exercise called the Red Candle Technique.

What I want you to do now is "see" in your minds eye, this is the 3rd eye, found between the two physical natural eyes and just a bit above the brow line. It's the place when you close your eyes and think of something that you can "see" it with your eyes still closed. Got that? OK lets move on.

The purpose of this exercise is to work on your own style of visualization, as well as teaching you control over your abilities. Work on this for 10 -15 minutes every other day if possible, while the 4-count breathing should be a daily practiced technique.

Here are the steps to this technique. However begin with 4-count breathing first, and then move into this exercise when you are ready.

With your eyes closed, visualize a table in the center of a darkened room.

Upon the table "see" a burning red candle in a candleholder. Look at the candle, see it burn, notice the wax dripping. Can you feel the heat of the flame? Can you smell it burning?

Notice the redness of the candle. Notice the flame, the many colors, yellow, orange, maybe green, blue, or white.

Allow the candle to burn in the darkened room, notice how it illuminates the room.

Now in your minds eye, lift the candle from off the table, about 6-12 inches. Allow it to hang there in mid air. Don't worry if this takes some doing, with practice it will come easier.

Replace the candle gently (don't just drop it) to the table in your minds eye. Look once more at the colors, smells feelings and such.

Return your attention from the candle to your 4-count breathing. Then return your attention to yourself and to the place you physically are. Then open your eyes.

Now is a good time to write down in your special notebook (that you have just for this class) anything you may want to remember about your first visualization experience. Did you 'see" better than anything else, Do you smell well? Did you just know it was happening? Write anything that will give you insight into your development or jog your memory later.

You're the only one who will read this so make it as long or as cryptic as you want. But write something, when you have developed your skill more you will enjoy going back and reliving this experience again, I know I sure did.

Class #1
Test What you have Learned

© Lady Wolfen Mists 2000

Use extra paper if you need to:

True or False

_____ 1. The Goddess is twice as important as the God in Wolfen Wicca.

_____ 2. Wicca is a Satanic based religion that involves blood sacrifices.

_____ 3. All Wiccans are Pagans

_____ 4. More men were persecuted than women were during the "burning times"

Short Answer

5. What is your view of the Gods role in Wicca, as you understand it right now?

6. Explain the Pentagram in full, include directions

7. Why do we meditate?

Multiple Choice

8. How many Sabbats are there a year?

　___ 6　　　　　_____ 12

　___ 8　　　　　_____ 13

9. The English used to burn what at bonfires in crossroads outside of town?

　_____ Toast and Tea　_____ Children　_____ Cats in baskets　_____ dirty clothes

Essay

10. Write a short paragraph on how your visualization with the red candle technique went.

Wolfen Wicca ®
Class #2

© Lady Wolfen Mists Jan.1998
revised 20

Class # 2 ;
Theory

    Grades & Ranks

    Points on the Goddess

    Points on the God

    Grounding

    Pathworking; What it is

    Wiccan Rede breakdown

    Law of Three

    Ethics

Practical

    Grounding exercise

    Arms of the Lady *(Optional-Use Kitaro Light of the Spirit here)*

Test Yourself

    Quiz-

    Do Arms of the Lady & Grounding -Write about it

Class #2
Ranks or Grades In Wicca

© Lady Wolfen Mists Jan.1998

In Wolfen Wicca we follow the following Ranking or Grading system. Each level denotes specific levels of completion and achievement. Not all traditions of Wicca follow ranks and of those that do not all are exactly the same. Yet I offer to you the generals, and the system we, in Wolfen Wicca, follow.

It should be noted that we are a secretive group and initiations are secret, as well as certain rites and ritual, reserved for specific initiation levels. We follow the "Keep silent rule" with heart and soul. We require that all things be kept quiet and not spoken of to others outside our tradition.

Mundane- a regular every day person with no magickal intent

Cowen level -a very un- flattering name, denotes not only a

Non-believer but someone who has already made their mind up, without hearing the facts. Often a religious zealot condemning "us" to hell without hearing what we really believe.

Pre-dedicant- One who is just learning and is hoping to

become dedicated to Wicca. Usually at least 2 ½ months of study. At this point you cannot join in monthly coven/grove (Esbat) meetings, unless invited.

Dedicant-One who has worked, under a teacher or sponsor,

for a total of at least 6 or more continuous months of study in Wicca. At this level you have earned the right to attend esbats (full moon) rites and become part of the working coven/grove.

Initiation 1st degree level- This is the traditional length of time for most coven/groves. After 1 year and 1 day of continuous study, this

is a year and a day after dedication is achieved, the dedicant is reviewed and can be made ready for initiation. This is not automatic the review is given, and the dedicants progress is considered, and if the sponsor or teacher feels ready then the dedicant is suggested for 1st degree Initiation. If the dedicant feels they are ready they enter the Neophyte level.

It is at this level that plans are made on what learning (lessons) and personal goals are to be met for 2nd degree level, as well as any general group requirements must be met. At 1st level you may attend all full moon rites and sabbats and initiate healing work.

2nd Degree level - Usually takes a minimum of 3-7 years. Here one is considered an adept. The goals set at 1st degree level are reviewed here, and some sort of positive contribution must have been made to The Craft, as well as any general group requirements must be met. This **must** be recognized by others in your coven/grove.

3rd Degree Level-After many years of continuous (minimum 10-15 years) of study. This level is sometimes never achieved. Here you are known as MASTER of your abilities. There is extreme dedication to the Craft and you do work for the benefit of the grove/coven on a daily basis. You will "know" when you are ready and your sponsor or teacher will talk with you about the responsibilities you are about to enter into (they are wide and varied), as well as any general group requirements must be met before you attempt 3rd degree initiation. Your coven/grove members will aid in your decision.

Witch Queen- This is a third degree that has had 3 or more covens 'hive" or branch off of her original coven. This is a rank that deserves great respect, esteem, and honor.

Other designations

Elders- Not based on any age or sex. Any elder is someone who loves their Faith completely and totally and serves the Goddess and God as well as the pagan community with all their heart. They usually are hard workers who attend and are involved above and beyond the norm for extended periods of time. Another way one can be considered an elder is if they have special expert knowledge of a specific area of paganism or a tradition. I like to think of at least 5-7 years of **verifiable continuous study** in a specialized area.

Croning- (also called Grandmother) This is the time in life usually 45 or older (post-menopausal) where a woman becomes very active in owning her wisdom earned over the years. At this time the woman is wise enough to take time to not only acknowledge her shadow side but to explore it. There may be ceremonies that mark this rite of passage, they can be coven public or coven closed.

This is a rite that is to be taken seriously as the woman moves into an honored position of Crone and makes commitments to the coven, to the Earth, and many other responsibilities. The Crone is very valuable to any pagan community because she is coming of Age and has much wisdom that is accessible.

Saging – (also called Grandfather) This is the male counterpart to Croning. For a male the rite of Saging is usually around 55-60. Like the Crone it is a celebration of wisdom earned.

Curious Souls

Class #2
Goddess Information-Points for all

© Lady Wolfen Mists Jan.1998

THE Goddess: Points for all

The Goddess is one of the central deities found in the craft. She has traditionally been described through poetry, metaphor, humor, music, as well sacred texts and human experience. She is in everything we see, feel hear touch sense and know. Often called the Great Mother, she not only understands but created all the great Mysteries, to which we as Craft members wish Initiation into. These Mysteries and the Bright Lady herself can not be understood or explained completely, due to the physical limitations imposed in this reality in which we live and the words we use here. So we use myths, stories, poetry and many other analogies and metaphors to explain in the physical what our Soul knows to be true on the spiritual and astral planes. So when you hear someone speak of the Mysteries they know but can never say aloud, they are not trying to be deceitful, misleading or evasive, they are saying that there are no words to fully explain what they know or feel. It is these secrets or mysteries that must be experienced, and felt, to understand the inner knowledge that is available to all.

We, as Craft members, attribute the Mother Goddess as holder of this information and it is through her that we can access this information, giving us a better understanding of the self and of all creation. It is in this belief system that we feel that the Goddess is ever there ready for each and every one of us to reconnect to Her Spirit at our own individual rate or time. Craft members view the Goddess as Mother of All. It is said She birthed the world from Herself, making the Earth a living connection of and to Her. The land is seen as a living part of Her flesh, the air is her breath, the water are her Tears (her own body fluids) The rocks, trees and such are likened to Her bones. Knowing this we see the Earth as a manifestation of Her power and a sacred place where all Living beings need to live in balance and harmony.

      She is a 3 in 1 Lady as she is considered to have 3 main aspects of herself. These aspects include the Maiden, Mother and Crone which are akin to the life cycle of a woman as she grows and matures, she is Maiden stage, Mother stage and Crone Stage a reflection of the Goddess within and the divine spark that resides there. The Goddess is also said to be the yin polarity/energy power in all creation!

Class #2

Goddess Information- Importance today

© Lady Wolfen Mists Jan.1998

THE Goddess: Importance for women today

WICCA has seen a resurgence in modern day as it allows for the female needs in religion. This is something that many mainstream religions have had a tendency to ignore. In these types of religions women are often seen as chattel, owned by their male masters. They are the ones who are responsible for enticing men into the evils of sex. This idea makes sex a dirty sinful act that must only be entered into to "multiply" the human population on this planet. It is definitely not to be for enjoyment or pleasure.

In WICCA women are returned to their rightful place as an individual, not to be owned by anyone, equal to men and deserving of the same respect given to all living things. Sex is seen as sacred and a gift for loving couples, not to be entered into a frivolous way, but in a deep loving sacred commitment to be enjoyed by both sexes, without the guilt and dirty sinful connotations labeled on it by the mainstream religious factions today.

Aging is also seen as a part of the circle of life. Patriarchal society, as we know it today, give little to no respect to the aging women (and at time the aging man). In fact aging is considered something to dread, old is equivalent to ugly and undesirable. Women and their bodies are expected to fit into the social roles written by men, young beautiful, not to smart and above all else submissive! The Goddess rips that whole idea to shreds. She inspires, encourages and liberates women to be who and what they are. Each stage in a women's life is seen as a facet of the Goddess. The aspects of the Goddess maiden, Mother and Crone are all aspects of growth and empowerment in a women's life. Through the achievement of these aspects a women is no longer limited to the economical social roles placed upon her. She can awaken and use her own mind, feelings, ideas and choose what type of spirituality works best for her! What a wonderful liberating power the Goddess gives us!

Further importance to women is the belief that the Goddess is a living entity. That upon Her awakening to full consciousness She felt lonely and created all things in creation from her own body,

making each of us a direct part of Her being. Taking this one step further is the validation that we as living being contain a part of the divine spark of the Bright Lady and are in fact all Goddess in our right. We have only to reach out, in the spiritual sense and reclaim that part of our essence. That part of Her within ourselves that has been there since our first creation and can be found in all levels of our being, physical, emotional, spiritual, astral/etheric.

THE Goddess: Importance for men today

© Lady Wolfen Mists Jan.1998

THE Goddess: Importance for men today

More and more men are making their way to the Craft. Many are dismayed, discouraged, and repelled at modem day society and social morays as well as the rules and doctrine of mainstream religions. They are feeling boxed in and overwhelmed at the social roles that they have been handed, being told what they should feel how they should act and what they should do as "real men". Many are looking to experience all facets of who they are both the male and female side. The Goddess allows for the feminine aspects of a man's nature to be experienced, without feeling that they have lost touch with their masculinity.

To some the Goddess acts as a mirror reflecting back into their lives healing feminine energies. Through a relationship with the Goddess, and in the end their own feminine nature, they can heal past wounds caused by denying these energies. With these energies found deep within they can heal any abandonment issues or needs not met as a child.

The Goddess symbolizes the eternal Mother who loves all of us unconditionally, a facet of love that many of us need to experience more often. Her nurturing love helps men (in this case) through their worst fears, and teaches that love and compassion is not for sissies but for all who are whole, complete and functioning people. The Goddess is an example of all that society forbids him to be, yet She encourages and leads him to experience the whole complete perfected self, that he (in this case) was intended to be!

Class #2

General Points on the God

© Lady Wolfen Mists Jan.1998

THE GOD: His Importance to both Men and Women today!

He is born over and over again from the Goddess, and as the Great Wheel of the year turns, so He grows in power and strength until He reaches his impending death and rebirth. His growth can be charted with the seasons of the year in equal measure and to the nurturing love of the Goddess. It is her power He draws from as He grows, and matures. He is a triple figure just as She is and His aspects are, Youth, Warrior/Father and Sage/Grandfather . These to like the Goddess stages mark the growth of a male.

The Horned God represents all things wild and free. He is all aspects of masculinity, the yang polarity/energy power. He can experience, give and accept love, look for His Higher Self (connect to His spiritual side), regain His primitive shadow self, become one with nature, be able to show anger and discipline without becoming a power play or cruel. Yet most of all He can feel His emotions in full without feeling a threat to his manliness. The God is a representation of all positive male qualities found in a society that allows for the creative spirit and a sensitive being. He can and does interact one on one in an equal relationship with out fear of anything. This is especially noticeable in the one and one interactions with other men and with empowered women, He still maintains his manliness, but can do so with respect and dignity and honor to all involved.

Many mainstream religions place the man in a higher more powerful position that that of a woman. With the male in such a place of power, the women is then subjugated and lowered in rank and value. Thinking this way many believe that WICCA is just the opposite. That women are placed in an overseeing position of power and the male becomes a "second rate" citizen, on a far lower status. Nothing could be further from the truth!!!! In WICCA Men and Women, Women and Men maintain an equal, interactive, interdependent strong status.

This structure is empowered by the interactions of the God and Goddess themselves in their interactions with each other as well as their interactions with us as individuals. This continuous harmonious and equal structure is imperative to the central tenets and core of Wicca. It sets up the foundation for Harmony, Balance and a deep respect for all living things.

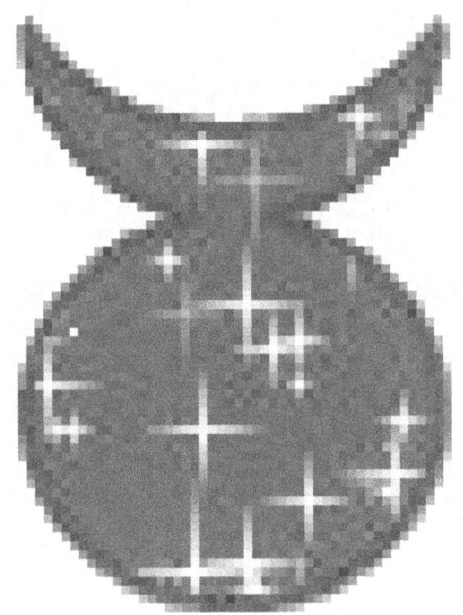

Class #2
Grounding; A basic understanding

© Lady Wolfen Mists Jan.1998

Grounding is that action that connects us to the Earth energies. It aids in making a clear link to ourselves, and the current physical energies that surround us. One needs to be grounded and well focused to accomplish anything in life and so it is much the same when working in magick.

Most magick, although appearing to be done on the physical realm, is often really worked on at the Higher Realms (astral/etheric realms.) To reach these energy planes (realms) we must often work outside of what we know to be the physical/material energy realm. It is here we direct our energies, thoughts, intents, and power to these other planes, and in the end this makes us very "ungrounded"

When we return to this plane (the Earth plane) it is important that we ground ourselves again. We need to call up the Earth energies and pull them back into our being. This avoids any side effects of working on other planes like;

1. Feeling outside of yourself
2. Feeling dizzy
3. Feeling confused
4. Headaches
5. Being tired
6. Feeling "munchie" hungry
7. Motion sickness
8. And so on

By grounding again you induce the following to happen;

1. You allow for a clearer memory of what occurred
2. You feel energized.
3. solid not flighty
4. Answeres and interpretation of events come easier you.

5. Solidly focused and in control on the physical plane.

6. As well as many other advantages

Grounding also helps in the storage of stray energies that may be brought to this plane along with you. If you ground such energies and direct them into a tool, such as a wand, then these energies will be available to you next time you choose to draw upon them. They will not just dissipate into the air and be gone, but can be an additional useful tool to you and your spiritual journey.

Class #2
Pathworking: Basics

© Lady Wolfen Mists Jan.1998

Pathworking

Pathworking is a really important part of Wicca and one I, unfortunately, cant render properly on paper. Pathworking is a narrated journey to or on the inner planes (astral/etheric levels.) However I do CAUTION you on this type of work, it should not be attempted by an untrained person, no matter how well meaning or how simple the journey maybe! You are attempting to use some techniques that deal with the mind and this could pose a danger if your narrator is untrained and unsure. What to do if circumstances that may be irregular arise. I am a Certified Hypnotherapist and have spent many years working, training and ultimately teaching these techniques so I know what I am saying when I caution you in this area.

Pathworking, for all that, can be a wonderful experience when done correctly. It can take you anywhere, anytime and still keep you safe. It can lift you up to the astral plane or to your safe place. In my actual "in class" classes we do pathworkings to the arms of the Goddess, Safe Place, To the Summerland, Visit with Guides, See specific God & Goddess aspects, Trips to Atlantis and on and on. I deeply regret I can't offer that to you here. Yes I could put it on tape but I can't see how you are reacting and I need to know that. I am also often "Goddess Inspired" and add extra instructions for each individual student, and that would prove an impossible feat here.

Qualities of a Good Pathworking;

The following list gives you physical qualities that need attention if the pathworking is to be successful for those involved. Pre planning is the key;

1. Quiet! That means no phones to ring (including cell phones or beepers) No Loud noises, TVs off

2. Comfort A comfortable place to sit or lay, comfortable non binding clothes, pillows available for those who want one, Blankets for all as body temperature falls when doing this. No watches or tight fitting jewelry

3. Scent There should be a nice soft smell in the air if possible, I love Nag Champa or White sandalwood. Just burn enough to scent the air slightly not to over power.

4. Soft Light Candle light is best but be careful with the open flame

5. Music Some thing emotional that sets the mood you are trying to create. It should be without vocals. I particularly like anything by KITARO especially the Astral CD he does.

6. Other things to remember: Tissues for everyone just in case, water in case of coughing, sometimes even cough drops for smokers or such if a coughing fit breaks out. Oh and another item I have learned to ask about is for those who have asthma, do they have an inhaler with them? Once a student had an asthma attack in the middle of one of these pathworkings and didn't have his inhaler, it was pretty scary and something that could easily have been avoided if we had been better prepared. So think over what may be necessary for a comfortable experience for all involved and try and make that available.

Class #2

Wiccan Rede Breakdown

© Lady Wolfen Mists Jan.1998

There are many different variations of the Wiccan Rede. Some are quite beautiful and poetic, others quite simple and to the point. I love collecting them and reading them. I place them in my Book of Shadows to review when I need inspiration. In the 200 level class book you will be given a copy of one of the longer forms of the Rede. But for now this short form is concise and to the point. This is an item you should know backwards and forwards and be carved into your heart and soul.

There are really few things that most Wiccans agree on, as many traditions teach different things, such is the beauty of our most adaptable religion. However almost all Wiccans follow 2 main premises.

1. The Three Fold Law (discussed elsewhere in this course)

2. The Wiccan Rede. We, unlike most mainstream religions do not have 'Thou shall not's" spelled out word for word. No we believe that each person must take a conscious responsibility for their actions thus the Wiccan Rede!

It is fairly simple to understand but at the risk of beating a dead horse I want to go through it line by line so you understand it completely and let its meaning be impressed upon your heart. Oh one more thing Rede means Law. Here we go; written in bold = the Traditional Rede. Written not in bold = my meanings for your understanding.

Bide the Wiccan Law ye must,

You must stick to this law to be truly Wiccan

In prefect love and perfect trust.

This is a reference to how you come to a circle, your mind heart and soul is open and ready to give and accept the perfect love and trust that will be found there. No back biting or hurting each other only acceptance and unconditional love

Eight words the Wiccan Rede fulfill,

The following 8 words are the key to the Law that must be kept to carry on the true meaning of being Wiccan, anything less is a break in the law and is not a true Wiccan behavior

And Harm Ye None...do what ye will.

And this is the crux of it all, do what ever you want so long as it doesn't infringe on another's rights, take away their ability to make choices or do them harm in any way. Remembering that anything you do in the universe is vastly interconnected to all other things, so behaviors and spell casting and such MUST be thought out and be in the highest interest of all involved and not just a whim in which you are helped and others are hurt.

Lest in thy self defense it be,

There is one exception to this and that's when its in self defense. You must decide if it self defense or not (that's your part of the conscious decision making and responsibility.) then you must use the very minimum needed to extricate yourself from the situation

Ever mind the 'Rule of Three!'

Always keeping in mind the rule of three in all things you do

Follow this with mind and heart,

Always keep this law written in your mind, heart and soul, keeping true to it

For Merry we meet & Merry we part,

Merry meet & merry part is a common greeting and goodbye of Wiccans meaning until I see you again may abundance and blessings rain upon you. Whence we meet again may it be only in Love and Trust and positive energies surrounding us

So Mote It BE!

Another common ending to sacred ideas or thoughts, ritual or spells meaning "It Will be So" or "I make it so," I will accept nothing less.

Standing Stones of Calanais

Wiccan Rede

Bide the Wiccan Law Ye Must
In Perfect Love and Perfect Trust

Eight words the Wiccan Rede fulfills
And Harm Ye None, Do as Ye Will

Lest In thy Self defense it be
Ever mind the 'Rule of Three'

Follow this with mind and heart
For Merry we meet & Merry we part,

So Mote It Be!

Class #2
Three Fold Law or Law of 3

© Lady Wolfen Mists Jan.1998

The Three Fold Law is another foundational item you must understand before we can move forward in your studies. What it does is basically put the responsibility for your actions or inaction's back upon you and not some great God head that takes the blame for you. It is an essential item found at the core of your beliefs and it says this:

The Three Fold law;

Whatever you do in this lifetime, be it positive in nature or negative, it will be returned upon you 3 fold (3 times as much.) If it is not taken care of in this lifetime, then it will be revisited to you in yet another life time, as much as ten (10) times as much.

So lets really think about that....Say you have a person who is in your way at work and you cant stand it anymore. You go ahead and do a spell to hurt that person deeply, maybe drive them crazy. Besides being a blatant breaking of the Wiccan Rede, you have also set yourself up for 3 times whatever pain you have sent to them! Ok so in some cases you can get through this life without paying it back, but in yet another life you will have to pay them ten times the pain you caused them. Think it over if you don't like them in this life your really not gonna like them when you have to experience the pain (10 times) as bad as what you caused them in this life. Is it worth it??? I think not.

This is a good rule of thumb ask your self over and over when in doubt, is this something that I need to become involved in. Is my action's going to be worth what may be returned to me? If the answer is No, then don't do it! Allow the universe to keep the balance of what is owed and what's due, they are much better at it than we are.

Now as for self-defense, this question always pops up. That again is up to you, if you feel that you were violated not that you need to tip the scales a bit then that's up to you. What you can do **without adding** to what's owed or due if you are afraid of becoming

wrapped up in this persons karma **is Invoke the Law of Three**. Its really very simple:

In a sacred place, light a red and white candle, also some pleasant smelling incense if you like. Now close your eyes and meditate, call upon the Lady and Lord, explain to them how you feel you have been damaged. What was done to you and why you feel the need for justification.(have plenty of tissues ready as this can be very emotional and that's ok.) Then ask that the Law of Three be invoked and that the perpetrator get their just dues soon. Then ask for healing of the situation so that you may once again feel the Lords and Lady's perfect Love and perfect Trust. That you may move forward in your life, and leave this violation behind. That you feel like the victim no longer but now a survivor, and a whole being once more. Then spend a few minutes listening and allow the Goddess and God to speak to you if they wish. Thank then for listening and thank them for acting in your best interest. Tell them you will accept what ever they deem fit and allow them to leave.

Just a side note: You can also ask that 10 times be invoked if you feel very strongly about it but I have always found it best to leave such judgments up to the Goddess and God, as they are loving and swift with justice and wisdom. So that's all there is to it, but as I said The Three Fold Law is essential to the core of Wicca and to your spiritual development until you truly understand and feel it within your heart you will have trouble moving forward. So study it and understand what it means to you as an individual, and as a Wiccan.

Class #2
Ethics: Lady Wolfen Mists Reprint

Lady Wolfen Mists Speaks on:

ETHICS

© 1991 by Lady Wolfen Mists,

This section is reprinted from my book, LADY WOLFEN MISTS PARTS THE MISTS, Dec. 1991. I feel that this topic, in WICCA, is one that is often times overlooked in terms of explanation for beginners and some (so claimed) advanced practitioners. With the media made "fad" towards Wicca I feel that this isn't presented as strongly as it should be, so it became my personal "mission" to try and provide an ETHICS guideline to any practitioner who may be seeking information in this area. Please understand that this is targeted for WICCANS and is not meant to offend any other pagan religions, such as Santeria. So with that in mind here's the total reprint!

Welcome to the section that I think is the most important area to you, the practitioner. It covers ethics! For those of you who read my first book this will be very familiar to you, read it again! I wish to explain my "ethical basis, " and what it means to you, the practitioner.

Let's say you wish to do a love spell on someone, to force them to fall in love with you. Now that's not hurting anyone is it? Isn't love the thing that everyone looks for? The answer is yes, love is wonderful, but forcing someone to love you isn't wonderful. In fact it's unethical!! Any time you try to take away another's choice, in any matter, you will end up harming that person, as well as yourself. There is a fine line between manipulation and orchestration

In a spell where you use manipulation, you deceive that person, or completely remove that person's ability to decide. However, in orchestration, you set up a series of events. These events allow you to be seen in your best light. This allows the other person involved to decide for themselves, without any coercion from you, if they wish to become involved or not.

So, as you can see, it's always good to think and rethink any spell you may be preparing to cast. What are the ramifications of a spell like this? Ask yourself if you are practicing manipulation or orchestration? Is this spell going to hurt someone, and pile up the negative karma for you?

There is yet another area I'd like to cover it's very basic to ethics. I don't feel this can be emphasized enough! So for those of you who have already heard it, listen again. This area is called the Law Of Three or the Three Fold Law. What this law states is that no matter what one does, positive or negative, it will be returned to the sender three (3) times over, and in some cases ten (10) times. So, once again, you need to ask yourself if you really need to cast this spell?

Are you acting in Self Defense or are initiating a situation? Would you mind if it was returned to you three (3) fold? **If the answer is that you wouldn't want this revisited upon you, then you are doing something that is most probably unethical!**

Then on a final note. When casting spells never use blood sacrifices!!! The Lady and Lord of Light would never call for blood sacrifices in any type of spell casting. Life is sacred and a gift from the Goddess and God, not something they would ask for you to return to them as a part of your spell casting. Any deity that calls for such sacrifices to prove your faith or value will only ask for more and more. If you indulge in such practices, your very soul may become twisted and perverted. Negativity then, may become the very core of your existence.

The keys here is if it "feels" wrong, don't do it! Listen to your intuition; it seldom will lead you in the wrong direction. The second key is are you indulging in manipulation, have you impinged on someone or something's freedom of choice? If you have, its unethical, no beating around the bush. It's just plain wrong!

Remember the Bright Lady and Lord find their praise in the healing works, and positive deeds done in their names. So, if you are ever ask to cast a spell that takes a blood sacrifice, I recommend that you don't. In fact, get away from these type of people requesting it, as quickly as possible. These are not the types of practices that you would want to become involved with!

So, keep your spellcasting clean and ethical. May you forever walk in the Light of the Loving Mother, and Her consort, the Great Lord.

Bright Blessings,

Forever In The Loving Service Of Others

Lady Wolfen Mists

Class #2
Grounding; Tree Technique Exercise

© Lady Wolfen Mists Jan.1998

Ground Tree Technique

After a pathworking, meditation or general circle (raising a cone of power) work you will need to ground and focus! Here is a wonderful Technique for grounding.

Once you have returned to your body or to physical consciousness. Sit comfortably with your eyes closed, take 3 deep cleansing breaths, in through you nose and out through your mouth. Visualize a clearing away from erratic or random energies that may be around from your 'trip".

***This step is optional; See your breath placing these energies in to a selected tool (IE. wand) to be called upon later as you wish. (End optional step)

Now as you are sitting there envision in your own minds eye al the parts of you touching the floor beginning to grow think dark roots, much like that of a tree. Feel your consciousness flowing down the roots, as these roots continue to grow and snake downwards, deeper and deeper into the warm softness of the Earth. You will feel the warmth of the soil and the sweetness of life and crispness of water all flowing over around and through you. Still your roots pull you deeper and deeper, past sand, bolder and clay. Go deeper still. Finally your roots find what they are looking for and electrical green energies flow up them and into you. Now these life giving energies that link you to the very essence of earth, and all the wildness there.

You feel the grounding energies of life at first contact as it spreads through you, into your feet. It flows up your legs, to your hips and groin over your stomach and lower back, moving very quickly now. The energies fill your chest, back shoulders arms, neck and finally your entire head with their electric green life energy. You

allow them to flow through you, moving through every cell of your body until there is no separation between the two of you. You are the grounding pulse of Earth's life force and it is you.

As you breathe out you see in your minds eye these green energies coming from you, you are one, total and complete; now you are linked and grounded.

You spend a few minutes drawing these energies into your physical self and bask in the wondrous feelings they evoke from you.

Now it is time to return to full physical consciousness. Visualize the energies moving back down your body, as they entered. Down the roots in to the earth, down they go deeper and deeper. Finally at the ends of their roots they return to the soil. Your roots begin to return back up to your body; with every breath you take they move closer to your physical body. Now take 4 deep breaths by the 3rd deep breath your roots will be back into your feet/body and you will be grounded, re-energized, and focused. On your 4th breath you will remember clearly all that you saw and will open your eyes ready to meet the physical world once more.

Note: When you return you may want to write in your notebook all that went on in as much detail as you like so that you have a record of your travels. Be sure to include all that you saw, tasted, smelled, heard, said, felt and so one. Later in your spiritual journey you will enjoy re-reading all that has happened to place you where you are that very day.

Class #2
Pathworking: Arms of the Goddess
(Optional Study)

© Lady Wolfen Mists Jan.1998

Pathworking

This is a narrative journey called a pathworking; I usually use it in class with my students. I recommend that you read it aloud in a tape recorder and listen to it while you meditate. I also recommend the most excellent music by ***Kitaro (CD/cassette) called Light Of The Spirit,*** if you are looking for "just the right" music.

(Read the following into a tape to meditate upon it)

What to do once you have called down the Light and allowed it to permeate your body, I would like you to allow the light to flow through you. In the place that it enters the body at the top of the head that used to be called the "soft spot" as a baby (known as the Crown Chakra) I would like you to focus your mind.

Feel yourself rising out of your body, moving up through the crown chakra. Feel your consciousness rising,...up....up....up. Moving out of the body and up the cylinder of White Light. Moving quickly yet feeling no fear. You move up the light. Higher and higher.

As you look above you, you see two lovely arms and hands extended through the clouds and they gently pick you up and cradle you. You feel safe and secure in the hands. The hands lift you closer and set you at a table.

It may be a grand round table or a simple picnic table or something in between you will know. Before you is a beautiful blue cup, it seems to glisten in the sunlight around you. You turn and before you stands a woman, perfect to you in every way. She offers you your favorite drink and serves you. You realize that the Great Goddess has just served you and it was HER arms that reached for you, HER HANDS that sat you here. You are overwhelmed at the unconditional love that emanates from HER.

Tears of joy spring from your eyes as She caresses your hair and rubs your shoulders, telling you all the while how happy She is that you have come.

She tells you how very special you are to Her. How proud She is of you and how you are right on time for where you are meant to be.

Then She leans over and whispers a special word in your ear. **LISTEN!**

She tells you how this word is only for you, not to be shared with anyone else. When spoken aloud or quietly it will take you directly to the presence of The God and Goddess. Where you can seek their council for whatever you need or just reside with them to renew your spirit from the pains of everyday life.

Spend a few minutes with Her alone now! *(Wait a minute or two)*

Now She bids you go, but tells you, you can return whenever you like, as you know the way. She lifts you gently, puts a soft kiss on your cheek. The scent of flowers (particularly roses) flows over you quickly and is gone.

You are back in your physical body, the white light is gone. Be sure to focus and ground, then write down your experience and your special word in your notebook

Homework Note:

PRACTICE THIS IN THE FUTURE BEFORE MOVING ON!

Return to the Arms of the Goddess by using your word at least two more times, ask questions or just sit with them both and get to know them and yourself better, you'll be glad you did.

This is your first trip; limited through it may be, to the astral planes. You will be safe with the Goddess and God and it will be good practice for you.

Class #2
Test Yourself

© Lady Wolfen Mists 2000

Use additional paper if needed

Short Answer:

1. What are the 3 names of aspects of the Goddess that are likened to the Growth & Empowerment in a woman's life?

2. Explain what a pathworking is?

3. Give your basic understanding of the Wiccan Rede and the # Fold Law?

Multiple Choice

4. What does the Horned God represent?

    ___ A. All things wild and free   ___ C. Both A & B

    ___ B. All aspects of Masculinity   ___ D. None of the above

True or False

5. _____ Ethics is important to a firm foundation in Wicca and Magick use.

6. _____ We ground so we can gain weight.

7. _____ In Wicca you can do what ever you want no matter what.

8. _____ In Wolfen Wicca you can be a 1st degree in less than 6 months.

9. _____ The Goddess is Yin energy and the God is Yang energy

Essay

10. Write a short paragraph/review on how "Arms of the Lady" and the grounding exercise went for you.

Wolfen Wicca ®
Class #3

© Lady Wolfen Mists Jan.1990
revised 2000

Class #3 (include colored tear out Chakra circles page)

Theory;

    Moon Phases

    The Foundation for Building (AKA the 4 cornerstones)

    The Pentagram, what does it symbolize

    Chakra; facts about Chakras

    Chakra points chart & Chakra Layout

Practical;

    Test

    Do a *General Chakra Alignment*, using the circles provided in the tear out sheet for the amount of time shown on the chart- Tell me how it went!

(Optional-Use Kitaro Light of the Spirit here if you want, music enhances the session)

Class #3
Moon Phases and Information

© Lady Wolfen Mists revised April, 1,1999

Whenever you work with magick, whether it is in spell or rite or rituals, you need to get an idea of the phase of the moon. You also need to know what works best in that specific phase. Knowing this and understanding the importance of working within specific moon phases helps to ensure success in your magickal endeavors. For this reason I have listed below, the most basic moon phases and what they are most often used for.

There are 5 types of moon phases listed here, but usually most practitioners concern themselves with **the 3 main**, which is **Waxing, Full and Waning**. These main phases correspond to the 3 aspect of the Goddess and the Stages of a woman's life. The other point I would like to make is that although moon phase is important, I often believe that somewhere out in this great universe, there is the moon phase I need to tap into. It is theses energies I focus on, and use to "spin" my spell off of. However, I warn you that this is not a traditional approach, but it has worked for me for well over 30 years.

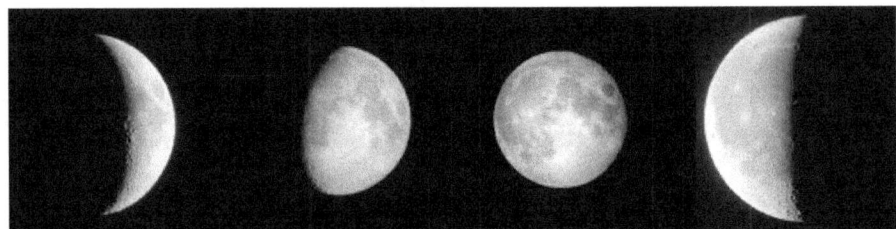

New t0 1st ¼   ¼ to Full   Full to last ¼   last ¼ to New

Moon Phase Period	Approx. Time	Rise/Set	Used to/for	Waiting
New Moon: Rebirth Aspect Return/Re-emergence	Best on day of New Moon but Can include up to 3.5 days <u>after New Moon</u>	Rise at Dawn. Sets at Sunset	This is a time to explore personal growth issues. To ask for healing's & blessings from God/dess. Spiritual exploration. Start new ventures	Magickal work in this phase often see results by the next cycles **Full** Moon

Waxing Moon: Virgin Aspect	Best on exact Night Rise at Noon Sets at Midnight Occurs between 7-10.5 days **after New Moon**	Good for attraction magic, building power in spell work. Good for power in spells like gaining abundance, success, love, luck, wealth, friendship, so on.	Magick endeavors in this phase usually see results by the next cycles **New** Moon
Full Moon: Mother Aspect	Highest power on the actual night of full moon. Rise at Sunset Sets at Dawn Can include up to approx. 14-17.5 days **after NEW MOON**	Moon At full Power, excellent for divination & protection, Psychic powers enhanced, healing of very serious conditions, time of x-tra power	Magick attempted on this phase may take at least a **Full cycle** (1-month to the next) for completion of works.
Waning Moon: Crone Aspect	Best on exact night Rise at Midnight Sets at Noon Can include up to approx.10.5- 14 days **after Full Moon**	Best time to work on banishing negative energies, returning power you have given away. Time to take this power back and rid self of addictions, illness or negativity. Work on lost self esteem	Magick endeavors in this phase usually see results by the next cycles **Full** Moon

Dark Moon: Death Aspect Return to Summerland Aspect	Usually occurs about 3 days **before New Moon Rise at** 3:00 AM Sets at mid- Afternoon **10:00 AM is the strongest**	Begin work on divorce, enemies, justice, any problems in your way, Spells to stop theft, stalkers & threats to you, friends & family Yet some traditions state this is not the time for magick and should be a time of reflection and meditation, its up to you	In the time it needs it will be done, if you're will is in harmony with the "best interest" of the Universe & all involved therein.

Why stress the Moon?

The Moon is seen as a symbol of the power of the Goddess, manifested. When "we" Invoke the deities for help or call in favors, like on the Harvest Moon, "We" are working with the physical energies set up by the Goddess, through the Moons orbit.

These physical energies are magnified to their maximum output at specific times in their orbit, thus the energies that eminent from it are used for specific uses and reasons. When you learn the Laws or conditions of each moon phase you will see a tremendous acceleration in your success in magickal results and in magickal aptitude.

This is another reason Wiccans meet on the full moon for Esbats. The Esbat marks the power emanating from the fullness of the moon and celebrates our dedication to the Great Goddess Herself; it is our worship time. Be clear that we do not worship the moon, only the power that the moon provides, that is seen as coming from the Bright Lady. This power or energies She sends us, marks our ability to meld with the Universe, and to produce particular out comes while tapping into the powers the moon is presenting to us. For example on a full moon healings are at their peak as well as protection spells.

Now with this in mind, you need to understand that the moons orbit travels through the zodiac sings. Doing this allows for specific influences on the astrological sign it is traveling through. For this purpose I have included yet another chart that marks these influences.

Moon In:	Dates	Specific Influences
Capricorn :	Dec. 22 - Jan. 19	Business, standing, honor, discipline
Aquarius:	Jan 20 - Feb. 18	Friendship, acquaintances, hopes, dreams, giving, humanitarian, human rights
Pisces:	Feb. 19 - Mar. 20	Development, evolvement, growth, karma, secrets revealed
Aries:	Mar. 21 - Apr. 20	Beginnings, self, personality, disposition, temper
Taurus	Apr 21- May 20	Financial/Success matters, benefits, All matter of material possessions
Gemini	May 21 -Jun. 21	Relatives, Beginning family, communication, intellectual matters
Cancer:	June 22 - July 22	Home, over sensitivity, death, family
Leo:	July 23 - Aug. 22	Love(give & receiving), entertainment, and hobbies (individual in nature)
Virgo:	Aug. 23 - Sept. 22	The environment (in general and in specific), health issues
Libra:	Sept. 23 - Oct. 22	Marriage, partnerships, all matters of law, justice
Scorpio:	Oct.23-Nov.21	Sex, lust, inheritances, legacy, major changes
Sagittarius:	Nov.22-Dec.21	Metaphysics, long-distance travel, religions, Looking for Higher self

Just a side Note:

A **Blue Moon** is when there is a full moon twice in one month. They are very powerful, great for Initiations!

A **Lunar Eclipses** symbolizes the perfect balance of both the sun and moons powers. You can attempt any type of magick at this time and be assured that there will be plenty of power to go around to aid in success. This success is due to the amplified energies that abound at this time.

Class #3
4 Corner Stones

© Lady Wolfen Mists Jan.1998

"4 Cornerstones"

To build a strong house to hold your store house of knowledge, you must first have a strong foundation. In Wicca this foundation is called the 4 Cornerstones. They are simple to understand and should become forefront in your memory. When in doubt of what to experiment with or how to conduct yourself remember these guiding words. These standards are meant as a traditional guide, by which too not only guide your learning experience, but to reflect your personal levels of achievement. Here are the 4 Cornerstones;

1. To Know:

Be sure of the things you know, it is not bragging or egotistical to be sure of your knowledge. However, do not be afraid to admit those things you do not know, as this is part of growing. Even the most knowledgeable is always gaining in knowledge.

2. To Dare:

It is important to be familiar with your abilities and to know your limitations. Yet do not allow your limitations to stop you from trying new things and testing your limits.

3. To Will

Do not be afraid to send your will out to the universe as long as it fits into harmony/balance of it all. This "will" would not break the "harm ye none" rule, so it wouldn't bind, bend or take another's choice from them. It would reflect the intention that 'if it be in the highest good of all involved, then let such & such happen." You would then release the built up power of that will (wanting such & such to happen) into the universe. Thus sending out your will and making magick happen.

4. To Keep Silent

It is important to remember that this corner stone is based on the many who traveled before us and were killed, tormented and tortured for their beliefs. To keep silent means not to talk about or reveal others you may know that are in the Craft, as this could cause them harm (i.e. loss of job, social standing, etc.) To reveal this information would also violate the Perfect Love and Perfect Trust code of the Craft.

Class #3
Pentagram

© Lady Wolfen Mists revised April, 1,1999

What About That Star That You Wear?

The Pentagram is one of the most misunderstood symbols that we have. To followers of the Craft, it is one of our most Holy Signs of Protection, sort of like the Christian Cross or the Jewish Star of David.

OK I understand that but what does it mean?

The Pentagram denotes all the elements of creation and the spirit of man, how they interact and are interdependent on each other . The top point of the star is Mans (meaning all humankind not just males) spirit, the following right point is water, then fire, then earth then air, coming back to Mans spirit. The circle that surrounds the star is the symbol of life, birth, and death and rebirth.

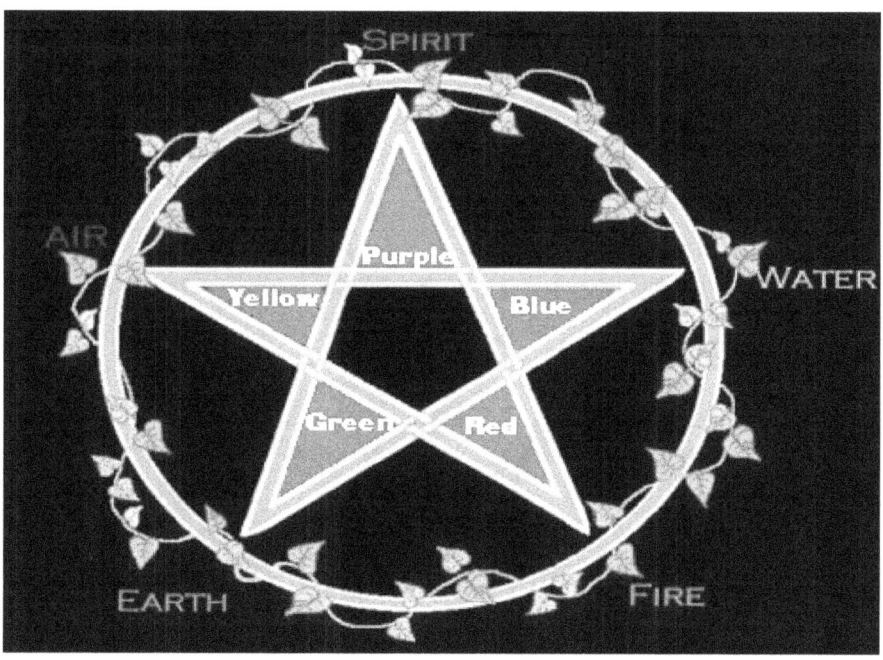

What does it mean when the star is inverted?

This is the part that has really gotten a bad rap. Satanists, and modern media as well as a few others that could be named here have taken this symbol and made it represent Satan. Yet to followers of the Craft all that an inverted Pentagram means is, coming from the spiritual plane to the material plane and brings those attributes with you. That's it, see nothing to do with Satan.

You may see another type of Pentagram, it shows a Pentagram right side up with a smaller one inside inverted. To followers of the Craft this means, As it is above, on the spiritual plane, so be it below, on the physical plane.

See it's not so scary once you really get the facts.

Class #3
Facts about Chakra's

© Lady Wolfen Mists revised 1999

Chakra is an ancient **Sanskirt** word meaning "the Wheel," and is often used in healing and astral work. The Chakra points are located throughout the body, and are used as links to gain spiritual/psychic information. For our purposes we will be working with the seven- (7) main energy or vibratory centers. These centers vibrate at certain levels, and as such, they are known to correspond to specific colors and stones. It should be noted that although the chakra's are associated with the Endocrine system of the Body, they are not actual physical organs.

The first chakra we will look at is the Crown Chakra. This Chakra is found in association with the Pineal gland. This is the SUPREAM Chakra, in that it has some control and knowledge of all the other Chakra points. Here one will find the center of the individuals spirituality. This center will deal with many issues like what is God or Goddess? How does one become one with the Cosmic Consciousness? What is my destiny in life? One must also be WARNED that this is the chakra that is most often used to "BIND." Binding is unethical and violates the three-fold law, but you need to be aware that this is the most common site that is attacked for the binding and controlling of you to another will. Psychic Vampires especially love this site as they attempt to drain you of energy and power. Be sure that you check and clear this one especially often.

The second chakra is called the 3rd Eye or Brow Chakra. You will find its body association is with the Pituitary Gland. Here you will find ones center of intuition and seat of creativity. This chakra is also said to hold the very development of your clairvoyance! This is seen as the site of abstract thought, by understanding and being able to work successfully in abstract thought ones consciousness is greatly widened and additional levels of the astral plane automatically are open to you.

The third chakra is the Throat Chakra and it is associated with the bodies Thyroid Gland. The Throat chakra is the center of communication. It is here that the ability to express oneself freely and without reservation is developed. If you were taught as a child to shut up and don't speak, this site may be a bit stifled and you may be unable to express yourself well. This is due to the blocks set up in childhood and needs to be address; cleansed and aligned so that you may truly be the functioning spirit the universe intended you to be!

The fourth chakra is the Heart Chakra and is associated with the Thymus Gland. It is in this chakra point that one develops the ability to love without fear and to accept love without fear! Major statement there, not just to give and take love but to do so without fear!!! This chakra is said to be the center of emotions, and in my experience it seems to be the one most people carry baggage around from. They carry memories and hurts of childhood, bad date, betrayal, loss, and humiliation, never fitting in, never being good enough and on and on. They lock these feelings away way down and then wonders why they can't seem to feel loved or give love unconditionally. Simply and purely this chakra point must be cleansed and the garbage put out! You must be able to be in touch with your emotions and feeling or else your not gonna have much success on the astral plane, where much spiritual work is done. So if you need to spend a little time checking this one out do it.

The fifth chakra is the Solar Plexus, and is associated with the Adrenal Glands in the body. This is the chakra point that works pure energy in the body and the continued balance of that energy. This is also the place where the persons "will" is found. Your force of focus and dedication to any cause can be evaluated here and worked with. If you have a weak will (i.e. cant stay on a diet, I can relate to this one) its here you need to explore the reasons for that particular weakness and what you can do it increase that level of your "will." The will is a might thing that is often over looked but you will want it in prime operating condition when you are ready for spell casting.

The sixth chakra is called the Navel Chakra or the Spleen chakra. You will find this chakra in association with the Pancreas. This chakra is know as the seat of Attraction (i.e. Luck love, cycles and so on) It is this chakra that attracts many things to you, hopefully in most of us it is good thing (like luck ad love) this is a

symptom of a good cleaned and energized chakra. Yet in some of us bad luck seems to flock to us and negative things continue in cycle, this is a symptom of a dirt and mis-aligned chakra that you need to work on. This same chakra aids you on picking up on the feelings of other, may can relate to saying "its just a gut feeling" Well in all honesty it's a navel chakra feeling working to tell you something, do well and LISTEN!

In addition to all this the Navel chakra works very closely with the Root Chakra developing levels of sexuality and what makes up your erotic essence.

The seventh, and final chakra we will discuss, is the Root chakra or Base chakra. This chakra is associated with the sex organs. It is from this chakra that the basics of survival instincts come from. Here we see the instinct to eat, sleep, procreate and be, it also set up the way so that we may grow and evolve and look to the higher realms. This is a very base and physical chakra. If one has a tendency to be a victim a lot this is the chakra that needs to be examined and worked on to find out why this happens and why this person needs to learn survival wise to improve their state of BEING. This chakra is also used to aid in the ground to Earth energy and the use of such energy, in purification and tapping into those energies whenever the need arises.

Basic Cleansing Information
What to expect

Each Chakra point can be explored individually or in a session. If you are having problems in specific areas, like you cant seem to use the gifts (occult wise) that you were given without fear. The first place to check out problems in would be the 3rd eye chakra. Once you clean that you may notice you need to also go to the throat chakra because there has been some 'bleed over" here from lessons learned that said you can't speak about your gifts so cleaning is necessary there also.

Even though each chakra point function independently of each other they also function as an interdependent unit and you can pretty much bet that id one is affected there are others that are also. So cleaning them all doesn't hurt.

What you may see when you go looking.

In a meditate state you will go into your self and see in your minds eye various wheels or windows of color. They should be clear and glowing (the color chart is on the next set if information) but chances are if you have never been there before the wheels or windows will be dirty and hard to see through. Some individuals report the images of ivy and tress and weeds growing over very dark windows. Each person may see something different, keep in mind each person is different and each experience is unique to the person. There are no right or wrong and each is as valid as the rest. The only point is that none or so broken or torn that they cant be repaired and cleansed and renewed. So no matter how bad it looks you (we) can fix it and you are not stuck.

You may also see large thick cables or vines (I will refer to such blockages and misaligned energies as cables from here on in) wrapping about the chakras, these are mis-aligned energies that are drawing energy off you or are binding you in some way. You will want to remove them.

Its easy first look at the cables and when you touch them you will know instantly who it is, why its there and what caused it. Its garbage!!! Get RID OF IT!

There are a few exceptions to this rule and that is that of a parent and child or such. This is a healthy relationship in which you are ok with them tapping into you and you want to participate. You will however want to attach this cable in a more appropriate manner, so it isn't choking you.

To remove cables;

While sitting in the meditative state physically take your right hand (hand of power) and no it doesn't matter if your left handed or not. The right hand is always the hand of power. Take your right hand and pass it in front of the chakra your clearing, see the energy of the hand cutting away the cables. Some people see a laser others see a saw others report such intense blockages they see the hand firing dynamite. It's all up to you; just remove the blockages and cables. Once this is done (I suggest passing the hand 3 times cleaning and slicing as it passes) you will notice the color returning to the wheels or windows until they glow the colors expected (see list on next section)

Once you have passed at least 3 times, do as many as you need but at least 3 times take the left hand. Pass the left hand over the newly cleansed chakra seeing it seal this chakra point. Some people report covers of quartz like watch faces, what ever works for you is fine just don't forget to seal. Sealing is a big thing, otherwise psychic bleeding takes place, and all you work is for nothing and you are open and run down!

How to reattach cables in a healthy manner;

OK lets say you have a cable that belongs to your family member and you want to keep it but it seems a bit big and draining. You shear it off like any other but then you pick it up once more and reattach it yourself. While you are reattaching it think on how you want it to work, any limits you want to set and how open you want to be. This allows for a clean connection and one in which you set the rules not one that is forced on you! Then move on just like you would any other cleansing.

What happens to the removed cables and blocks?

They are sent back to the sender or the person that put them there. You are freed of such influences and they are aware you no longer have the connections they forced on you. Sealing is imperative here or they can reconnect.

    Another issue here is cleaning up and taking out the garbage, especially in the heart area only to wait a few days and pick it all up again. Why would someone do this after all that work? Because they feel different and maybe a little alone. They are uncomfortable with the new unblocked potential and although they may not like how it was they understood it and were comfortable with it. This new potential is scary and they don't know the rule. Listen close now, here the secret to it….There are no rules to figure out! You make them now, you are in charge and no one can force you if you don't let them. So weird as it may feel, scary as it may be there is no failure here, just learning! Don't pick up the junk and garbage, let it lay and continue to move forward! You have made a mighty step in releasing, cleansing and aligning chakra's, be proud of yourself. I'm very proud of you ☺

Chakra Point	**Healthy Color for identification in cleansing**
Crown	Rich Vibrant Purple
3rd Eye	Deep Starry Indigo
Throat	Wonderful Sky Blue-or Electric Blue
Heart	Rich Emerald to Forest Green Can be Apple Green also
Solar Plexus	Sunny Golden Yellow
Navel	Orange, Like the fruit deep yet intense
Root	Red, like a deep red rose or red wine

    I also want to note on this chart, this is just a guide. The colors mentioned are the true chakra colors however the shades may vary from person to person. These shades are the ones most often seen by students and masters alike and are the ones I use. Yet if you see a different shade, and it seems that the chakra point is as clean and as aligned as possible, that may be the true shade for you.

    But as I said these are the most common, often when other shades are reported the individual has over looked something or something is being held back that they are not ready to deal with on an emotional level. **Don't push**, if the body/spirit/soul doesn't think you are ready emotionally then wait. It knows what is best for you and when it's the best time for you to remember with the least amount of emotional/physical pain.

Class #3
Chakra Layouts and Points on Body

© Lady Wolfen Mists Jan.1998

The following layouts have been specifically designed for beginners. They are for self-use and I strongly caution using them on another, especially the healers layout. The main reason for this is you simply don't have enough knowledge in the physical/astral/etheric levels to initiate healing as yet, and this could run into some real problems when dealing with others. However you are fully aware of your own reaction and feelings when working on yourself.

The <u>General Chakra Alignment</u> is needed before you successfully move on to the next steps in the classes, so please do this at least once a month. The "in class" students must go through a pathworking where all chakra points are cleansed, aligned and energized. It is a very emotional class, as years of garbage we carry with us is thrown out and replaced with positive loving energies. As this would be difficult to do in a correspondence class I have included the chakra alignment, which is the very minimum needed to move on. Yet if your ever gonna be in the area it would be worth your time to make an appointment (fees vary) for a professional and total cleansing, alignment and energization.

Here is the placement of colors and the chakra points they correspond to as well as time limits you will want to follow when doing an alignment. Oh before you ask, no you cant over clean so if you feel led to do this say every Sunday or so that's fine. It's a wonderful habit to get into as it makes everything in your life a little more balanced and you will feel/see a tremendous difference when its done often.

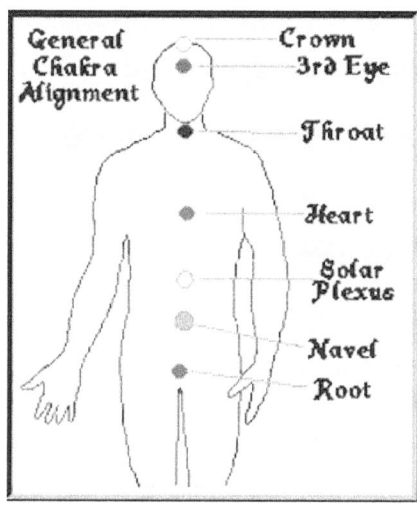

General Chakra alignment

Do this at least once a month with Colors and Treatment Time

Crown	Violet	10-15 minutes
3rd Eye	Indigo	5-10 minutes
Throat	Blue	*Not more than 5 minutes as it totally relaxes the body
Heart	Green	5-10 minutes
Solar Plexus	Yellow	5-10 minutes
Navel	Orange	5-10 minutes
Root	Red	*Not more than 5 minutes as it stimulates the Physical & Astral Body

Steps: Start at crown and work down. Place color swatches on each chakra point for the allotted amount of time. When removing Blue & Red at end of 5 minutes, replace with crystal (clear Quartz) or white Circles until time to remove all color swatches.

The *Self-Healing Layout* is a general overall activation of the bodies' natural healing energies. Through the use of stones and the properties they contain these healing energies are awakened to any

illness or obstruction to the natural flow of energy. The stones then 'break up" the obstructions or mis-aligned energies and replace them with balanced harmonious energies. Stones are wonderful tools in healing; this exercise is also designed to acquaint you on a beginner's level, with their many possibilities.

Steps to the Self-Healing Layout

Remove stones from the salt bowl that has had enough salt to completely cover all the stones. Make sure the salt bowl is only used for this purpose and the salt inside the bowl can be used over and over again. The salt cleanses the stones and makes them ready for use.

In addition to the seven (7) chakra stones used in this lay out.

You will want the following;

       Two (2) Ritualized Quartz

       Two (2) Agate (Botswana works best but
              any agate will do)

One (1) Bell

One (1) type of Incense & matches, as well
              as the appropriate burning device
              to place the burning incense in.

On the following page, is your chart to follow for placement, type of stone both traditional or non, times and points of interest.

An important note before starting. Start your session at the Feet and work up, when removing stones start at the crown and work down.

Placement of stone	Type of Stone & Time Length
***Both Feet** (on top or bottom) *This is an optional stone(s) for enhanced grounding.* Place one on or close to each foot **Time 15-25 minutes**	Traditional: Agate I Like: Botswana Agate
Root Chakra **Time: 10-20 minutes**	Traditional: Any Red stone I Like: Rhodonite
Navel Chakra **Time: 10-20 minutes**	Traditional: Any Orange stone I Like: Carnelian
Solar Plexus Chakra **Time: 10-20 minutes**	Traditional: Any Yellow stone I Like: Citrine
Heart Chakra <u>**Caution here:**</u> Do not use Aventurine here unless you know the person doesn't have a heart condition as aventurine has to much energy and causes heart problems in those with heart conditions! **Time: 10-20 minutes**	Traditional: Any Green Stone I Like: Bloodstone (gentle flowing energies) or Emerald (another soft flowing energy) Caution when using Aventurine as it is full of fast moving energies and may cause irregular heartbeats
Throat Chakra **Time: 10-20 minutes**	Traditional: Turquoise or any Blue stone I Like: Cherry Tigers Eye (also called the actors stone, which is great for ideas, feeling & communication skills) or Turquoise
3rd Eye Chakra **Time: 10-20 minutes**	Traditional: any indigo Colored stone I Like: Amethyst as it is the stone of psychic energies Higher Self, hidden mysteries

Crown Chakra **Time: 10-20 minutes**	Traditional: Rock Crystal I Like: Hematite, it has memory protection and is a highly reflective. It has a record of whose been messing around the crown chakra.
***Both Hands,** hold in both hands This stone(s) is optional for magnification of energies. Place one on the palm of each hand and hold gently, loosely **Time: 10-20 minutes**	Traditional: I Like: Rutilated Quartz magnifies 10 times the other stones energies that you are using

After 10-20 minutes remove the stones, starting with hands, crown, 3rd eye and so on, ending with the feet. Then place all the stones back on the salt bowl and submerge completely in the salt. Next take the bell and ring one time at each chakra point. This action signals the body the healing session is complete and the chakra's are sealed. If you don't want to use a bell, which is the best way, you can use the smoke from a sacred incense. Allow the smoke to encircle the body for 2-3 minutes. This also signals the body the healing session is complete and all the chakra's are to be sealed so you don't have psychic bleeding.

What is psychic bleeding? It is when there is a rip or tear or open point in the aura or etheric body, thus these energies bleed out of you in a constant stream. It gives you that "beat up" run down feeling. You know the one where you go to sleep and awaken the next morning feeling tired and beat up, yet you slept all night (8 or so hours) and can't figure out why you feel so bad. You are probably having psychic bleeding and need to heal it. For minor rips and tears from everyday stuff or minor skirmishes on the astral plane you can use the *Self-Healing Layout* to heal these. For worse rips and ears you may need to seek professional help which include auric needles and etheric body repairs.

Class #3
Test Yourself and what you have learned

© Lady Wolfen Mists 2000

use extra paper if needed

Short Answer;

1. Why are the cornerstones important to us as Wiccans?

2. Explain the 3 phases of the Moon and how it relates to a woman's life?

3. Explain in full what the Pentagram means and why it's important to Wiccans?

Multiple Choice

4. Which Chakra is most often used to bind one to another?

___ A. Heart Chakra   ___ C. Root chakra

___ B. Crown Chakra   ___ D. None of the above

True or False

5. _____ The Blue Moon is the 3d full moon in a month.

6. _____ To pagans the inverted pentagram is a sign of Satan.

7. _____The waxing moon can be used for attraction & abundance spells.

8. _____Turquoise is often called the "actors stone".

9. _____ The third chakra's color is deep forest green.

Essay

11. Write a short paragraph/review on how the healing and alignment went for you and place it in your special book.

Wolfen Wicca ®
Class #4

© Lady Wolfen Mists Jan.1990

revised 2000

Class #4

Theory;

    Blessing & Curse for your Book

    Book of Shadows and Grimoire

    Magickal Names

    Minor Tools

    Major Tools

    Record Keeping-List all major tools

    Candle Dressing Handout

    Safe Place

    Path work of safe place   *(Optional-Use Kitaro Light of the Spirit here)*

Practical;

    Test

    Meditate on what your safe place may be like

Book Of Shadow Blessing & Curse

By Lady Wolfen Mists ©1999

In this book that I do write,
Are the Mysteries of the Hidden Night.
Darker than the Velvet Sky,
Sweeter than the Sun up high.

Blessing all who enter here,
Invited by the Lady near.
Those who Hearts are but to Share,
With Purity and Honor there

A boon I call from Hecate!
"To destroy and cast away
In 3 fold form those that steal!"
The circle turns the Karmic Wheel.

© April 1999 written for Auction BOS   Side note ; the line "Invited by the Lady near..." refers to owner of BOS, if the owner is a male change to Lord near)

Class #4
Book of Shadows and Grimore's

© Lady Wolfen Mists revised 2000

You may commonly think of witches with cauldrons and big old dusty books that contain all manners of spell and rituals. The Media has firmly planted this image in our heads. But what is a book of shadows and what is its true function?

Book Of Shadows

A Book of Shadows is a sacred book that traditionally belonged to an entire coven. Only the High Priestess and the Book of shadows Keeper were allowed to write in it or access it. In it were rituals, rite, spells, recipes and so on the coven worked on. There was also a record of information important to the coven and its members like a records of Wiccaning's/Paganing (like Christian baptisms), Handfasting's (like marriages), Go of the ways (like divorces) Crossings (funerals) members achievements and ranks and so on. You get the idea. Everything that was important to the grove/coven was written here.

Grimoire

A Grimoire on the other hand was a personal collection of information, usually in the owner's own handwriting that often contained much of the information given above, but only on a personal/individual level.

Yet today we often use the terms interchangeably. Individuals now have a Book of Shadows (BOS) and you hear the term Grimoire less and less. I find either use acceptable as such I leave the decision up to you, the individual. Whatever term you chose you should also understand that many people break down their sacred book as it can often grow large and cumbersome. Such broken down parts are often referred to as "leafs." Such leafs may cover areas like dream work, or ritual writing or recipes or tarot. Anything that you feel deserves its own volume. There is no limit to the "leafs" that can spring from your Sacred Book. Your book can be simple or very elegant.

It can be a 3 ring binder you decorate or a bound volume, it's all up to you. I like the 3 ring binders best as I am always finding little tidbits I want to add in different sections to my Book of Shadows. Another important point is many traditions still make their students copy everything in their own handwriting.

All information and teaching **MUST** be written in the dedicant's handwriting copied from the grove/covens main book of shadows.

In Wolfen Wicca we do not follow this practice! I just don't see the point, with so much information out there and with the use of type writers, copy machines and the internet I feel that handwriting such information is nothing more than busy work and a waster of students time. Information that has not been handwritten is often easier to read, gets out to the student faster and allows the student to gain information on a much quicker and more complete basis than those of years gone by. Heck some witches now keep their sacred book on computer disk. Who am I to say this isn't valid. If it helps you learn, if it teaches you and provides you with a relationship with the Lord and Lady, and if you use it to work with the light then by all means do what works for you!!!

A few things your BOS or Grimoire should have in it;

1. A blessing and curse on the front-page warning those who look without your permission.
2. A index system (I like the ones with the tabs on the sides so you can easily go right to the area you want to look at. Others like an involved page number system with a table of contents.
3. A table of contents isn't a bad idea at all it lets you know what's in this leaf if you have more than one.
4. A special pen (or two, pencils are ok also) used just for writing in your book. These should never be used for anything else
5. A section of blank and blessed paper for your use when needed.

6. A section to write all that you experience in your safe place, name all the items you store there, who gave them to you and what they may do. Any Spirit Guides you meet and animals that live there.

7. A section to write about your visits to the Goddess and God- all they say to you, all they give you and the times you share together

8. A section for other astral work or dream work.

9. Other sections for spells, rituals, recipes, and so on. Get the picture?

This class (Wolfen Wicca 101) is a book of shadows in itself and can be indexed as one. Since you need a Blessing and a Curse in your BOS I have included one for your use. Feel free, in fact I encourage you, to write your own down. You can use this one on the following page as it is or as a guide!. It should be placed in the very front of your book, the first thing someone might see.

Class #4
Magickal Names

© Lady Wolfen Mists revised 2000

Magickal names. You hear them all they time, they often sound greatly mystical and mysterious. But what are their purpose really? Why have them? How do you get them? So many questions, lets try to answer a few.

Magickal names have many reasons. I am not going to try and explain every traditions reasoning behind magical name, but I will explain our (Wolfen Wicca) We ask that our member adopt a magickal name because it aids acknowledging to the student that they have made a life changing commitment. That they are no longer the same person they were before and are now on a spiritual path. We do not ask that they give up their birth (mundane name) as this has its place in their world also. The magickal name is used in the context of magickal gathering and in reminding them of the spiritual creature they truly are.

A magical name should mark the progress of an individual, it should reflect who and what they are. It should have deep spiritual significance to the student and to the God/dess. For example I had a student who chose the name Rising Sparrow. He felt that a sparrow is a common humble bird, not in any negative sense but in the sense that we are all sparrows in learning. He liked the idea that his spiritual quest was lifting him from where he was to where he needed to go. He studied hard for a few years and his study rewarded him. On his first degree Initiation name changed from his dedication name of Rising Sparrow to Lord Dragon Seeker, a great jump from a sparrow to a most majestic and spiritual creature, full of ancient wisdom and understanding.

Another student wanted to start right out at the top he wanted Dragon Rider to be his dedication name. Yet it did not reflect who or

what he was at the moment. It didn't show his essence or his learning achievement. He was eager to learn but wanted it all RIGHT NOW! We talked about what he was interested in, where he wanted to go and how much time and energy he wanted to dedicate to his quest. Then we came up with a dedication name that seemed to fit for the time, Little Lizard Walker (something that makes you smile with the promise of things untold to come into being.) Maybe later he would earn the right to be called Lord Dragon Rider, but right now it was not to be so.

One must always show respect to those animals and objects that you incorporate into your name. Respect is a key here as you are choosing to represent these animals or people or items and as such you must do your up most to do so in a way that would bring honor to not just yourself but to the individual who's name you bear.

In Wolfen Wicca we do not allow any one below 1st Degree Initiation level to use the Term **Lord** or **Lady** before their names. It is a symbol of rank and attainment and something to shoot for. Also we do not allow any one below 1st Degree Initiation level to take the name of Gods and Goddess's. It is our tradition that the Goddess, through the High Priestess gives you your 1st Degree Initiation Name, this is your coven use name and as such is sacred and recorded in the Book of Shadows.

Pre dedicant and Dedicant's are expected to pick out their own names. They can continue to use that name but their new 1st Degree Initiation Name will be added to if. For example as told above here is how it would be announced; Lord Dragon Seeker, the Rising Sparrow if Lord Dragon Seeker had chosen to keep both names.

Different kinds of magickal names;

First off there are many different types of names do you need them all, of course not. Can you use them all if that's what you want then so be it.

Here we will look at the 3 basics uses of magickal names. They are as follows;

          1. Public names

          2. Coven Names

          3. Sacred Soul names

Public names are just that, names one uses in public. They are magickal and what most people use in interviews or at gatherings or in the public eye. My public name is Lady Wolfen Mists, almost everyone who knows me knows me by this name, in fact most people know me by this more than they know my mundane (birth) name.

Coven names are names that just your coven sisters and brothers knows you by. This would be the coven/grove you regularly practice in. This could be a special official name or a nickname, but is just used within the coven and just those close to you know it or are allowed to use it.

Sacred Soul Names are names that you discover or are given to you by Spirit Guides or the Bright lady or such. They are sacred and hold much power and should never ever ever be shared with anyone, they are your soul name and should be guarded with your life.

The Power behind a name;

You may think what's the big deal behind letting someone know your name, I mean its just a name. However you don't understand the magick behind it. It's not just a name it is who you are, it is part of your life force and a piece of your very soul essence. We believe that if you can put a name to something, anything including a person and you speak it out loud you can manifest what ever you want surrounding that name. For example if I knew your soul name and I was unethical I could say something like. *Universe hear me, I call into being great trouble and pain for (your soul) name. I have said it so mote it be!* Now depending on my ability to focus, concentrate and send my will out I may have just sent you a bunch of trouble and you cant figure out what's going on. I can also use your name to access your energy, your power and your gifts...so you can see there is MUCH power in knowing a name, guard yours well.

Now is time for another personal story about my soul name, If your not interested skip this section.

****
Begin Personal Story

Many years ago I was very ill after a spiritual battle I was ill prepared for, and some friends were helping me. One was cleaning me with specific stones while another was drawing pentagrams on me

to seal in the positive energies. While this was going on I felt as if I were spinning out of control in a free fall. I was very sick and in my minds eye I saw a great Golden Eagle fly directly at me.

It was so real I tried to lift my arms to ward it off, as I was sure it was about to tear me apart with its open talons. I screamed and it flew right into me, but instead of tearing me to pieces it wrapped its wings about me and lifted me from the place I was falling to. I could see it, smell it and even hear its thoughts. I had never seen a power animal so clearly in my life I could count the feathers and see the dots in its eye.

I spoke to my friends telling them this was the coolest thing, this eagle just came out of no where and was flying off with me, they continued to work on me.

I began a conversation with the eagle, it seems a bit put out by my most recent actions, as I had just went into spiritual battle with someone who was much more experienced than I was and this sickness was the result. I could tell it was displeased at my sorry attempts and it made it clear I needed much more training before I try something on that level again. It was sarcastic to say the least but one thing in particular was that it gave me a name.

Me, thinking it was the eagle's name shouted it out to my friends who were still working on me. I will never forget how my eagle cocked its head at me and said, "That's not my name stupid its yours and stop telling it to everyone or you could be in danger of losing your very soul!"

It then told me how I could use this name in the future to draw power from when I did battle, to wrap myself in the armor of my soul name and as such I would become almost invincible to negative energies. That there was much power in my soul name as it was the compilation of all the experiences my soul self had ever had. Not just me, Lady Wolfen Mists now, but all the persons I had even been.

Well needless to say that was many years ago and I have learned a lot from my eagle since then, always blunt in her lessons she has taught me much. Not the least of which is to keep my mouth shut until I know what's really going on (big accomplishment for me).

So now I hope to relate you the same lesson of how very important a soul name is and how you should guard it with your very existence.

****

End Personal Story

Picking the right Name for you

How do pick the right name for you? One way is to list names or items or colors or whatever that you are drawn to. Ask the Goddess to direct you? Look at where your interest lies in Wicca and go from there. Write down why you choose that name, what it means to you and why you feel it fits you. There is no right or wrong way, what else is new couldn't be simple right. No it has to do with going inside yourself and seeing what's there. Allowing the God/dess to guide you and you won't go wrong. A second popular way of coming up with a name is through the use of numerology.

Numerology & Names

Steps to checking your Magickal Name is numerically correct;

First you must check your birth number to see if your name is correct for you with regard to numerology. To do this follow the steps set out below.

1. Find your birth number. If you were born on February 2, 1959, you would find your number like this 02-02-1959= 2+2+1+9+5+9= 28

2. Bring this down to a single digit : 2+8 = 10

3. Then your birth number is 10

4. Then find the name number of the magical name you have chosen. Equating all the letters of the alphabet with the first nine numbers using this table does this.

1	2	3	4	5	6	7	8	9
A	B	C	D	E	F	G	H	I
J	K	L	M	N	O	P	Q	R
S	T	U	V	W	X	Y	Z	

5. Perhaps you have chosen the name Lady Wolfen Mists, (I included the lady as I worked for it, but if you don't have a title in front that's ok, just use the name you chose.) By using the above chart write out your name and figure out the correspondences:

L A D Y   W O L F E N   M I S T S
3 1 4 7   5 6 3 6 5 5   4 9 1 2 1

total numbers = 62 = 6+2=**8**

6. Now 8 on my magickal name does not equal the 10 of my birth number so this is **NOT** a perfect match, I must some how add 2 . Perhaps another t in Mists. So its spelling would read;

L A D Y   W O L F E N   M I S T T S
3 1 4 7   5 6 3 6 5 5   4 9 1 2 2 1

Now it's a perfect ten (10) same as my birth Number. For me this is just way to much work and takes the fun out of it but for some this is a wonderful and acceptable way of picking and spelling their name.

If you are unhappy with the new spelling of your name then you need to pick one that you would be happy with. As you can see this method may take sometime until you find something you would be happy with.

Now some of you may be wondering why it should match your birth name number. This is because this number is a constant in your life and not one that is open to change, its solid and will exude

an unchanging vibrational pattern around you, giving you strength of conviction and force of will. Not a bad place to start your magical birth.

As I said this method is way too mathematical and locked in for me, I'm given to more intuitive practices but either way is valid. So go with what works for you, as this is your magick and you know what works best for you

Time for another personal story. Again if you don't want to read it just move on

****

Begin Personal Story

How I got my Magickal name

I was trying to find a magickal name, something cool. You know like Crystal Star Walker or Light Spirit or Rider of the Violet Ray. Something real metaphysical and mystical. I was trying so hard (maybe to hard) to find just the right names that would represent me to the community. I was having a heck of a time. So I went to the Goddess and asked for help, yet nothing came for quite a while. I must say here I was never big on wolves at this time, I like dolphins more and Gorillas and big cats much more. I mean wolves were ok but not really my cup of tea.

Anyway one night in a dream (the Goddess contacts me a lot through dreams) I found myself in a swamp, the moon was high and there was much mists all about. I was not frightened but I was apprehensive. I walked down an old path. It looked as if Louis and Clark were the last ones to pass this way. I

could hear owls and frogs and crickets. There was a panther crying in the background. I jumped.

Out of the mists (which were getting worse by the second) stood a huge wolf. Almost all silver with emerald green eyes it beckoned me to follow, no words I just knew.

We walked a long ways and then the mist cleared. I was in a clearing and before me sat the wolf, behind him was a stump with a book open on it and candles on each side of the stump. A quill pen laid across the book and the wolf nudged my hand.

It led me to the book. I picked up the quill and set it to the paper in the book I wrote the name Lady Wolfen Mists- teacher. The wolf howled as did a pack far off and I became Lady Wolfen Mists.

I would have never considered such a name, but I was told later that because I am a teacher I have Wolfen Blood, blood for

teaching others, and I came out of and part the mists for others. Not what I would have expected at all but what the Goddess gave me and uses me for.

As for my name its not some huge mystical production but it is who I am and I would never part with it, it explains me better than I ever could. It is me, Lady Wolfen Mists it's a perfect fit. Oh and I love wolves now I just add then to my long list of critters.

Class #4

Minor Tools

© Lady Wolfen Mists Jan.1998

The following is a list of other tools you may want to collect also. It is by no means complete or exhaustive in nature. It's just meant to point out a few and give you direction in your search.

Altar Cloths: Various ones for different rituals, Sabbats and Esbat. We use a plastic table cover on our altar cloth as it helps keep the cloth clean and catches candle drips. There's nothing worse than using your favorite silk cloth then cleaning up, only to find candle wax or oil in the silk. The plastic seems to really help.

BOLINE: A Wiccan ritual knife used for more practical purposes, such as cutting herbs, etc. *never* to draw blood. Generally white handled with a curved or sickle blade, but can be any shape.

Candles for altar: In Wolfen Wicca we use 2 candles red and white on the altar. Other candles can be used later for other purposes but you need at least one red and one white candle.

Candle Holders: At least 2, big enough to fit the altar candles.

Candle Snuffer: Simple to snuff out candles, blow out a candle shows disrespect to the fire element. Snuffing is better.

Censer or Thurbile: A censer is an incense burner. There are many types. I like screen burners as you can use them to burn granular incense, adding the incense and making the smoke rise when you need it instead of a steady burning stick incense. A heatproof container used to burn incense.

Charcoals (Self-igniting) for granular incense: Must be used with a screen burner and a fire resistant plate

Food Platter: We have 2 of these. One is small and placed on the altar the other is larger and is used to serve the coven from on cakes and wine. It is not sat upon the altar if there isn't enough room a small table is sat up in from or to the side of the altar for Cakes and wine.

God symbol: (statues are nice) To honor and symbolize the God

Goddess symbol: (statues are nice) To honor and symbolize the Goddess

Incense: Various incense, to be used in rituals, and in circle.

Incense bowl: for granular incense on altar. This sets in front if the burner and is easily accessible to add incense to the burning charcoal when needed.

Matches or lighter: These should only be used for circle/coven work and stored with other magickal items.

Music: Various tapes or CDs that help set the mood for your ritual or Sabbat or Esbat. Be sure you have something to play your music on also.

Robe: This is ritual attire that is worn in the circle and at other festival occasions. In Wolfen Wicca there are specific colors combinations that can only be worn by the High Priestess and High Priest. You may have several robes for different occasions and Sabbats.

Sea salt- Used to purify the area and the energies raised

Salt and Water Bowls: Must be able to hold water for altar

Soap (Sandalwood purity): Use this to wash with before doing any magick or rituals. Help to remove any negative energies that may have collected during the day. Great stress remover. Specific bath salts (like purity) can be used in place of soaps.

Water Pitcher for altar (optional) We us this to pour "wine" from in a coven situation. Everyone has their own cup (usually paper) to drink from. As some are uncomfortable drinking directly from the chalice after another has.

Still other tools you can collect if you want to be used at different time for different reasons

Bell: Can be used to mark the beginning and end of a spell or ritual, to invoke the Goddess, to ward off evil spirits, and to invoke good energies.

Broom or Besom: Used in the actual "sweeping away" of any negative energies so that the circle is cleansed and made into a sacred space.

Cauldron: The cauldron is a "pot" used for cooking and brew making. It should be made of iron, stand on 3 legs. Traditionally the opening should be smaller than it's widest part and it should have a lid.

Stones: Various types for a variety of reasons

Herbs: Various types for a variety of reasons store in a sealed jar and in a dark place to last longer.

Oils: Various types for a variety of reasons store in a sealed jar and in a dark place to last longer.

Plus just about anything else your mind can think of, Happy Hunting ☺

Class #4
4 Major Tools

© Lady Wolfen Mists Jan.1998

In Wicca there are tons of tools one could collect to use and to work with but these are the main four you will need for the Altar, and seeking them out is half the fun. There are a few things to keep in mind when looking for tools. I never ever haggle over the price. It puts negative energies into the items and causes problems in the future. If you want it then buy it,

if you cant afford it then put it back, it wasn't meant for you.

Another tip is that your item need not be new, sometimes the best tools are second hand or ones that already have energies within them (positive of course). So junk shops are great, thrift stores, flea markets, just go where you are drawn and if it speaks to you and feels right to you then get it. Oh and before you ask, yes you can have as many tools as you like. I have many different wands, chalices and such for different occasions and for different uses. Some I knew right away what I would use them for, others I just got cause I liked them. Still others I got because someone some where may need it. So don't be afraid to collect!

Now with all that said the following information is given on each Major Tool is just a guideline. I have added the traditional expectations of the tools but don't get real hung up on that, just refer to it if you like. Heck I have the coolest wand that lights up and changes color. When the lights are out you can see the colored light trail it leaves as I invoke the Pentagram in the circle. Its make of plastic with fiber optic strands on the end, far from traditional but really cool and dramatic. So go with your intuition and let your creativity flow!

Quick Reference:
The Traditional Qualities of the 4 Major Tools

The Wand:

Traditional size from tip of middle finger to the elbow

Traditionally made from Hazel, Almond, Rowan, Oak, Holly Traditionally.

Wand is Unisex in Nature

Direction- East

Element -Air

Covers Wisdom of user, Imagination, Used by Elder witches to measure your abilities, tells of any new gifts or growth in user.

Athame (Ath-hame / A-the-May / At-Tame)

Often considered the most powerful tool because traditionally it is used to cast the circle (however I prefer to use the wand for circle casting)

7-9 inches with double blade for Black handle, Can be single edged or sickle like for White Any Material, but one Black handle & one White handle, Bone is neutral for color and silver or wood can be substituted for white

Masculine in nature

Direction- South

Element- Fire

Often represents the male aspect and is used in symbology as the God upon the altar.

The Chalice

Traditionally 6-8 inches tall traditionally

Can be made of any material, but wood or glass is traditional, pewter (lead free) is also nice

Feminine in Nature

Direction- West

Element- Water

Often represents the female aspect and is used in symbology as the Goddess upon the altar.

The Pentacle

Can be made of any material, Traditionally made of wax, to be easily cast in to the flames if trouble came. Leaving no evidence of worship but wax drippings.

No evidence = no prosecution

Passive in Nature

Direction- North

Element- Earth

This is a symbol of mundane forces of nature. Its the foundation of Harmony, a protective shield, aids ability for one to ground and center.

Class #4
Record Keeping

© Lady Wolfen Mists Jan.1998

In the future you will want to remember the special points on the items you collect. You may find yourself having several chalices for several different reasons. Your wands may be many and you may have collected several Athame's over the years. Each one important to you for its own reason and having its own story.

To help you remember when where, how and why you picked up this specific item you may find it useful to have a record keeping system. This is so many years down the road, when you're an old forgetful witch like me, you can open your Book of Shadows, go to your record keeping area and look up that special information on the special tool you just had to have.

On the following pages are empty record keeping sheets for your Major tools as well as non titled ones for your minor tools. I suggest you do not write on these but use them as master copies for your own Book of Shadows. Fill them out as detailed as you can, it may seem silly now as you can recall all the information without a problem, but who's to say in a few years. You may kick yourself for not writing that little story down or the exact impressions you got when you picked up that Pentacle or so on. So trust me on this record keep though monotonous is essential to remembering and focusing on use several years down the road.

Class #4
Record Keeping

© Lady Wolfen Mists Jan.1998

Item; _____

Belongs to (your name)_____

Item Name;_____
_____

Item Found; (Month, date, year)_____
_____

Place located;_____
_____
_____
_____

Uses For this Item;_____
_____
_____
_____
_____
_____

Any Interesting Information;_____
_____
_____
_____
_____
_____

Storage (Special way or in special color);_____
_____
_____
_____
_____

Other;(special markings or such)_____
_____
_____
_____

Class #4

Wand Record Keeping

© Lady Wolfen Mists Jan.1998

Item-- Wand

Belongs to (your name)_____

Wand Name;_____
_____

Wand Found; (Month, date, year)_____
_____

Place located;_____
_____
_____
_____

Uses For this Wand;_____
_____
_____
_____
_____
_____

Any Interesting Information;_____
_____
_____
_____
_____
_____
_____
_____

Storage (Special way or in special color);_____

_____
_____
_____
_____

Other;(special markings or such)_____

_____
_____
_____
_____

Class #4

Athame Record Keeping

© Lady Wolfen Mists Jan.1998

Item-- <u>Athame (black handle)</u>

Belongs to (your name)_____

Athame Name;_____
_____

Athame Found; (Month, date, year)_____
_____

Place located;_____
_____
_____
_____

Uses For this Athame;_____
_____
_____
_____
_____
_____

Any Interesting Information;_____
_____
_____
_____
_____
_____

Storage (Special way or in special color);_____

_____
_____
_____
_____
_____

Other;(special markings or such)_____

_____
_____
_____
_____

Class #4
Chalice Record Keeping

© Lady Wolfen Mists Jan.1998

Item-- <u>Chalice</u>

Belongs to (your name)_____

Chalice Name;_____
_____

Chalice Found; (Month, date, year)_____
_____

Place located;_____
_____
_____
_____
_____

Uses For this Chalice;_____
_____
_____
_____
_____
_____

Any Interesting Information;_____
_____
_____
_____
_____
_____

Storage (Special way or in special color); _____
_____
_____
_____
_____
_____

Other;(special markings or such) _____
_____
_____
_____
_____

Class #4
Pentacle Record Keeping

© Lady Wolfen Mists Jan.1998

Item-- <u>Pentacle</u>

Belongs to (your name)_____
_____

Pentacle Name;_____
_____

Pentacle Found; (Month, date, year)_____
_____

Place located;_____
_____

Uses For this Pentacle;_____
_____
_____
_____
_____

Any Interesting Information;_____
_____
_____
_____

Storage (Special way or in special color);_____
_____
_____
_____
_____
_____

Other;(special markings or such)_____
_____
_____
_____
_____

Class #4

How to Dress a Candle Handout

© Lady Wolfen Mists 1990

Imagine this, you're all set up for your candle spell, the circle has been cast, you have your altar ready, the candles set out, the incense going, music plays lightly in the background. The lights are off and moonlight is streaming through the open window. The power is electric and flowing though the air. You are 'charged' and ready to do your candle spell. You reach for your candle and read the instructions that are lying out on the altar. The instructions say; "Dress your candle with oil." You stop! The mood begins to falter, you loose your concentration on the spell. All that keeps racing through your mind is, "What is Dress your candle and how do I do it????"

I have been asked that question by many a practitioner of the arts. So here's a handout I give to students who don't know how. Hope it clears up everything.

Once you have chosen a candle for the spell you intend on casting, you will need to take time to "dress" it. "Dressing" a candle is fairly simple task, and should be done to EVERY candle you will ever use. The reason for dressing a candle are two fold.. One is to remove any existing energies that may be in/on the candle. Two, to place the images, energies and qualities within/on the candle. That way you ensure a higher percentage of success with your spellcasting.

Before dressing your candle you will need to obtain some oil for this specific purpose. There are many types of blended and essential oils you could use, be sure you pick one that best represents what you want in reference to the spell you will cast. If you are unsure of what oil to get that best represents your spell, I recommend something like Goddess Rising Oil or Blue Roses or Sandalwood. Any of these can be used in all forms of positive magicks.

The next step is to take some oil and dab it on your finger', then go clockwise around the middle of your candle to make a complete ring of oil on it (step 1 below). During this think of God/dess energies pouring from you into the candle. "See" in your

minds eye, the oil flowing from you into the candle. Know that what you seek in your spell will come true, that you will accept nothing less!

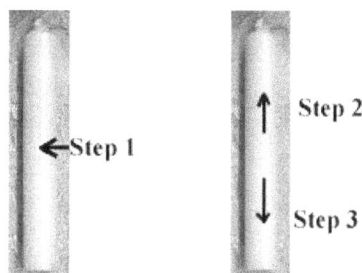

Once you have done this then pull some of the oil upwards toward the wick, (Step 2 above)once again in a clockwise manner, until you encircle the candle again. Continue to empower the candle by "seeing & knowing" the energies are flowing through you to the candle. Feel the power grow within the candle as every stroke adds the knowledge that your candle is now being filled, more and more, with your wishes and intent.

The last step in dressing a candle is to pull the oil down from the center to the bottom of the candle clockwise once again (step 3 above). If you are like me, you may feel the need to add more oil at this time cause there doesn't feel like there's enough left on the candle, just add more. But be sure that you place the oil around the center first, like at the beginning, and then draw it down in the same clockwise circle. Be sure to concentrate once more on what you want the outcome of your spell to be

Remember to send as many positive energies into the candle as you can muster up. The key to success with any candle spell is to **<u>VISUALIZE & CONCENTRATE!!!</u>** Now once you have visualized, concentrated, and instilled into the candle all the qualities you can. Once you have visualized the outcome of your spell and know that it will be the way you want it to, then you are ready to begin your spellcasting. Your candle is dressed and ready to go.

      One last note, many people have asked me if you can use a candle you have dressed for another spell if its not burnt all the way down. There are no hard and fast rules here, you can if you cleanse the candle very well and re dress it for the next spell. Yet be warned your success rate may be lower as it has already been used before and those energies may remain and send the spell off focus a bit. I highly recommend that if you are doing a spell use new candles for that spell, it allows for a higher success rate and the candle is much easier to impress your wishes and intent upon when its fresh and not used. But then that's my opinion, you do what works best for you. After all its your magick no one else's!

Bright Blessings,

Forever In The Loving Service Of Others

Lady Wolfen Mists

Class #4
Safe Place

© Lady Wolfen Mists revised 1999

What it is

Your safe place is that place within the astral plane that is your sanctuary. It's just for you, no one else! It is created by you to fit your needs. It is also called your Astral Temple by some people. It is not a physical site in the sense of something like your back yard on the physical/material world; it is a place where you can go on the Astral/dreamtime plane.

What it's used for

Your safe place is just that, a place that is safe and secure for you. Where you know you can go and experience the astral realm without worry of attack or invasion by those you don't want there. Such a place is used for Astral Healing and for connecting with Spirit Guides, a place for Power animals to dwell. You usually have a home of some type there and you can store you astral items there, everything from books to gifts to stone and such. It can also be used to set up a temple to honor the God and Goddess. You name it and if you can think of it you can do it in your safe place, without worry or fear.

Maybe people use their safe place as a sanctuary from the stress of everyday life, it heals and invigorates them and re-powers their souls. When I worked as a social worker in child abuse I would often come back after an especially difficult case and meditate for a few minutes. Going to my safe place and cleansing myself of all the negativity. I would re-power my soul and re-new my convictions. Such actions got me through many cases that would have emotionally torn me apart. I have also used it after a hard day of not being able to rest or maybe to satisfy my boss. It keeps me sane in the face of much stress and balanced, a necessary place that I alone could walk.

Where it's at & what's it look like

As I said before its located on the Spiritual/Astral plane. To get there you must be able to focus your energies and leave your body, rising to the higher astral levels. You need only to think of your safe

place and your emotion of wanting to be there will direct you there. Its simple, lay back go with the flow, that means don't analyze, let the images flow and Poof! There you are in your own safe place. If you have trouble use the visualization much like the <u>Arms of the Lady</u> in lesson #2, only see yourself going to your safe place instead of into Her Arms.

What's it look like? Well for each and every person there is a different and unique safe place. Some students report an underwater dome, other have just a meadow with a large tree, others report gardens or castles in the sky. You name it and it can be someone's safe place.

What will yours look like, no one really knows not even you till you get there. Shall I tell you the story of my safe place? If you are bored by personal stories you can jump down to the next section.

****

Begin Personal Story

Ok it was like this, I wanted a really neat safe place. Something with lots of flash and stones, ya know real castle like with lots of rooms and velvet and big chairs and marble. Just a spectacular fairytale castle, nothing hard about that ☺. I was sure that fit me, lots of drama and flash, so me!

When I got to my safe place I couldn't believe it. It was a small cabin, one main room, with a hand made rope bed. It has a long wooden table, again hand made, with a large fireplace that has a big cauldron hanging in it. There are herbs hanging from open rafter and few rugs around, there was a stack of firewood to the side of the room. Outside there are flowers and a thatched roof. In the yard sits an old gypsy like cart and a white horse grazes off to the side. There was nothing spectacular to the eye, no towers at all or large doors with unicorn statues to guard the way. I was so disappointed!

This **could not** be my safe place it just didn't fit my personality, or me. Where were the gemstones and the glitz? Where were the huge libraries or the velvet and wonderfully tooled furniture? No this had to be a mistake! I don't grow flowers (I don't like dirt or anything for

that matter on my hands) and I don't want to live in a gypsy cart ever! I went back inside and explored more. It was all as it looked before, 1 big room, no castle.

I began to poke around looking at things. Picking up jars and smelling herbs that were drying, finally I made my way to the fireplace, it was huge. It covered almost one whole wall, and noticed the cauldron. It hung on a cast iron arm meant to swing over a fire. For some reason I move the cauldron out of the fire pit on its arm, and noticed a different colored stone I touched it!

BOOM! The back of the fireplace opened up into a fantastic house. Marble everywhere, rooms with all my stones and library books on built in

bookcases that went to the ceiling, on and on. This was truly me. What I wanted and needed.

The front was a place for me to work hands on with nature, making my oils and such, I like to do this but I must have a place to clean up. Yet deeper inside my cottage lay the heart of what and who I am, here all I ever needed to learn and store things in was easily at my reach, in abundance as I had asked the Universe for so many times before.

The Goddess knew what it was I needed more than I did, and created for me this amazing place for me to go and feel safe in. I am a Spirit Warrior so there are times I need a place to safely recover from battle in, this is my safe place and I have learned to love it dearly. I use the gypsy cart to travel to the sea or to the mountains or to where ever I need to go, singing my heart out as my horse pulls me to my destination!

End Personal Story

****

So what's your safe place gonna look like, who knows till you get there. I have even had students tell me that they built their safe place. When they got there they just thought of the materials they would need and poof! The materials came and they created exactly what they wanted.

So for each person it is different and just as valid as the next. But I caution you on expectations (as I had many) allow the Bright Lady and Lord to guide your needs and see to what you truly need. I would have never considered a place like mine, yet after all these years I would never give it up; it is truly my safe place, my temple, my shielded sacred ground.

Who can enter it?

Anyone you let enter it! No one you don't let in can come, no one can break in, and above all else **NO ONE** (No thing) can do you harm there ! **EVER!** Got that? You are virtually in the womb of the Goddess when you are in your safe place and nothing, no one, no energy or such can touch you there or do harm to you or any one or thing you have stored there. It's just impossible! Cant be done, and don't let anyone tell you otherwise.

Now you will see lots of activity in your safe place at times, your spirit guides on all levels may be coming and going. Those who you call friend may visit. The Lord and Lady may visit as well as your power Animals and spirit protectors. So there you have it the basics on your safe place. There is one more thing I recommend. Immediately after your first visit to your safe place write down everything you saw and everything you did. If you're an artist draw a picture, even if your not an artist do it no ones gonna see it but you. Then put this is your book of shadows so you can always have a record of your first visit. Yes some say this old crone is somewhat sentimental, but its nice to some days revisit what it was like the first time through your beginner's eyes ☺

Wicca 101

Class #4

Path work of safe place

(Optional-Use Kitaro Light of the Spirit here)

This is a short pathworking to your safe place. It can be used with music or not, that is up to you. You may find it easier to record this pathworking and play it for yourself, then to try and remember it. The times are approx. how long you are to wait **after each** small section is read.

To my safe place

© Lady Wolfen Mists 1991 All right reserved

1 minute   Start tape if you will be using it Now.

Relax and being your 4 count breathing, allow the stress and strain of the day wash away from you. Breath in relaxing Light and out all those pains and stress that follow us each day. As you breathe in the light and out the strain of the day feel your self becoming more and more relaxed.

1 minute   Then begin to pull down the light as you have done before. Allow it to flow into the crown chakra. Feel it flow down the neck to the shoulders, relaxing you and healing your pains. Let this light flow through you, let it encompass you, becoming one with you.

1 minute   Feel the light flowing down from the shoulders and splitting down both arms. Feel it gently coursing down both arms to the elbows, from the elbows to the wrists. Allow this comfortable and relaxing energy ebb through your fingertips. They may jump or wiggle a bit as the light course through them.

1 minute	Return your consciousness to your chest area, feel the light wrap around you and go down...down....down the body.... to the waist to the pelvis. Let it sit there for a moment as the buttocks begins to relax as well.
1 minute	Feel the light fork down both legs, relaxing the thighs, to the knees, to the calves, to the ankles, to the feet. Focus you attention to the toes and like the fingers feel it flow through with light. Your toes may jump or twitch as this happens. That's OK, just continue to relax.
1 minute	As this light flows through you completely and out of you see it in your minds eyes , turn upward from your fingers and toes to surround you like a cocoon. You are now a being of light, totally encase, there is no difference between you and the light. The Light is you and you are the Light
2 minutes	As you become this light feel your spirit rise up and continue up the shaft of light flowing through your body, Higher and higher you go....Baking in the Love and Light of the Goddess. Rest in the cradle of her Hands as you rise up this shaft of light.
1 minute	Notice the clouds above the hands as you continue to rise, breaking through them you will see a hallway, you will go to the left. Walking down the hall until you find yourself on a landing. Before you is a giant portal. You will notice the scenery keeps moving. A beach front, a mountain, a valley, maybe a scene of other planets and on and on.
1 minute	Choose the scene that calls to you the most, the one you like best and step through the portal.

1 minute	Now go ahead and explore your safe place, knowing that nothing can hurt you here.
2 minutes	At this time I would like you to stop whatever it is you are doing and go to the door or entrance of your safe place. Before you, you will see and energy beginning to swirl and form. It may be white , blue, green or any combination of these. It will make contact with you, touch you or talk with you. It may just give impressions or a knowing of what it is feeling. It WILL give you a gift of some type. Take it even if you are not sure what it is and thank the being.
1 minute	Place your gift in your safe place home for safe keeping. Once you have done this please make your way back to this time and place, back to this room and into your body once more. Know that if you leave things unfinished at your safe place that is all right because now you know the way there and can return on your own at any time.

Now that you have returned be sure to ground your self. Also be sure to write this experience down with the date so you may have a record of your 1st encounter with your safe place and one of your first spirit guides, that who you encountered in the swirling energy, to place in your Book of Shadows.   End tape.

Class #4
Test What you have learned

© Lady Wolfen Mists 2000

Short Answer;

1. What is the difference between a Book of Shadows and a Grimoire?

2. What is the importance of a Magickal Name?

3. What are the four main tools found on the altar and the direction each represents?

Multiple Choice

4. The chalice was traditionally made of?

   ___ A. wood   ___ C. silver   ___ E. A & B
   ___ B. glass   ___ D. stone

5. A Boline is

   ___ A. Used to cut herbs   ___ B. used to cast curses & hexes
   ___ C. Usually has a bone handle ___ D. A & B
   ___ E. A & C

True or False

6. _____ A Grimoire usually belonged to the entire coven.

7. _____ Dressing a candle aids in successful spellcasting.

8. _____ You can let anyone in your safe place.

9. _____ A Soul name is your secret name used only by members of your coven

Essay

10. Write a short paragraph/review about your journey to your safe place.

Wolfen Wicca ®
Class #5

© Lady Wolfen Mists Jan.1990
revised 2000

Class #5

Theory:

Things you NEED to know

Dressing for Circle; what to wear and such

Pre circle Preparation; Personal Sacred Time

Incense with charcoal granular, stick or cone

Circle Casting Directions

Banishing the circle

Invoke & Banish Circle Quick reference Handout

Invoke & Banish Pentagram Quick reference Handout

Altar Set Up- Wolfen Wicca Style

Cakes and Wine ritual

Make Purification Sachet

Practical:

Do a circle casting write in your Grimoire how it went

Test

Class #5

Things you need to know for circle casting

© Lady Wolfen Mists Jan.1998

Circle casting is a sacred place you create to work magick. We don't often have physical sites like buildings or churches to practice our religion in so we create them wherever we need. The circle casting is a ritual you will need each and every time you do any type of work. Everything from coven ritual to spell work at home. It insures a positive energy place that is cleansed purified and consecrated to the Lady and Lord.

I have included a ritual for group circle casting but it can easily be adjusted to fit individual circle casting, you just take on all the parts.

However when circle casting you need to know what direction to go and what to do for this I have included handouts on circle casting and circle banishing. Casting always goes in a Deisol (pronounced Jes-el or De-o-sil depending where you're from) fashion (clockwise) starting in the East and working to the North. It is here you lay down the boundaries for your circle. Banishing is always done in a Widdershins (counter clockwise) fashion and it is the taking up of the energies put down. Starting in the North and moving around to end in the East.

Let's talk about the circle itself. The circle isn't really a circle at all, its more of a sphere that surround us completely It is like stepping into a bubble that you created and can mover around in. All time, as we know it stops there as we move to work on a higher astral level. Do not EVER just walk through the boundaries of a circle as it 'blows" the energy within it and all power escapes and other energies (maybe those not wanted) enter uninvited. If you must leave the circle

early or have to go to the bathroom (something you should always do before circle) go to the circle caster and whisper you need to leave. He/she will take the Athame and slice you a whole to slide through and then zip it up. If you return, wait to be let back in before barging through the walls.

Another area you must have knowledge of how to do is the invocation and banishment of the pentagram. Now this is handy not just in the circle but anytime you want a little boost in energy or a protective shield. I use it when there are people I don't like being around, it shields me from their energies. I use it when I have to walk to my car on dark night alone. I use it on job applications (invisible of course) to get the interviewers attention. When I was in college I used it on tests to keep up my grade point average. I use it all the time, everywhere not just the circle. Its something that should become second nature to you much like the Wiccan Rede.

I have included handouts on the way we in Wolfen Wicca invoke and banish the pentagram, but I know many of you will have questions on this. Yes you have seen it done other ways and yes those ways work to. There are about 100 different ways to invoke pentagrams and a pentagram for just about everything you can imagine from different Elementals one to those who help break a shopping habit. But for now as part of your basic foundation we will use this one. Its something we can all have in common when we practice together, use the others as you will in your private practice, but get to know this form?

OK lastly I have included a handout on Wolfen Wicca Altar Set up. This is another area where there are about a million ways to do this, each sect or tradition adjusts it to fit them and their tools. This is the one we like. It works best for our needs in Wolfen Wicca. However that doesn't mean that someone's else's form isn't right for them. Respect their ways if you wish to have your equally respected. So memorize this as best you can, it's the form we will use for most of our ritual in the following classes.

See following Handouts for Details:

Invoking Circle, Banishing Circle, Pentagram Invocation & Banishment, Altar Set up

Class #5
Dressing For Circle ; What to wear & such
In the Tradition of Wolfen Wicca

© Lady Wolfen Mists Jan.1998

Dressing & readying for Circle

4. Robe Vs. Sky Clad
5. Special Jewelry
6. Color of Robes
7. Stripes on the Sleeves of Robes
8. Wearing Awards
9. Footwear

There are several things to consider when getting ready for going to a circle meeting. Here are just a few major topics and suggestions.

1. Robe vs. Sky Clad?

Many covens/groves have specific types of robes that are allowed in a circle, as well as colors. Yet there are other covens/groves that practice completely naked, also called 'Sky Clad," within a circle. This is viewed as non-sexual but coming before the Goddess as you were born. This is valid and completely acceptable for those who are comfortable with this practice, and is a common practice with many European Covens.

Our tradition of Wolfen Wicca doesn't allow for "Sky Clad" for several main reasons. Here's the short-list;

> 1. Most of us seem to have "body hang ups" and appearing naked with a group often takes away from the ritual rather than enhancing the experience. This is because so many of us would rather be very self-conscious over our nakedness, and would be focused on that, instead of the intended ritual work.

2. Magickal Robes aid in the setting and ambiance of the circle. This allows the mind to go into "Magickal mode" and helps enhance the focus and energy flow of the circle and gives a very dramatic surroundings and environment.

3. Wearing Robes is strictly my preference and since I created Wolfen Wicca this is the way we do it. If you are practicing outside "Sky Clad" the bugs bite you more than with a covering (i. e. a robe) Sitting in the grass is more comfortable in my opinion, than naked (you don't have to sit and worry as to where the bugs may have crawled up into, 'nuff said ☺) Also I live in North Dakota and it gets COLD! Outside naked (often subzero) is just plain stupid no matter how many bonfires you light. One side will freeze, as the other side will toast. With robes (over your regular clothes) you can at least stand it for a bit.

4. Naked outside = problems with the law! Many people would see this as indecent exposure, not as a religious activity. Since many of us live in a city, and not on rural farms or such, neighbors may see this as a problem and call the police. This would not help in gaining creditability for our religion or ourselves. It may only add to the "crazy devil worshipers" stereotype that so many have already labeled us as. Now that's not to say that on private land or at places that allow for "Sky Clad" you cant join in if you feel like it. It just means that's its not something that we in Wolfen Wicca do often.

2.Special Jewelry

Most all practitioners have or collect Sacred Jewelry for the circle, to be worn in honor of the Goddess or God, or to show significant rank.

For example in our tradition there is a specific type of pentagrams that is given to various degrees. In this case a 1st degree initiates pentagram is worn to mark there rank as 1st degree. No one

else in the coven is allowed to wear this special pentagram within the circle except the 1st degree.

Here is a list of common jewelry that is attributed to ranks of achievement, and can only be worn by those who have achieved this rank, with in Wolfen Wicca.

> Crowns; Crowns are reserved for 2nd degrees only
>> both male and female

> Swords; Swords are allowed and worn only by
>> 3rd degrees

> Amber & jet Necklaces; are only allowed to be worn
>> by the High Priestess or crones within the circle. This is traditional as it marks the rank of High Priestess or Crone

> Garters; Usually with 3 or more buckles, can only
>> be worn by the Witch Queen, no one else

However any other type of Sacred Jewelry can be worn into the circle and will draw circle energies into it. These energies can really power up the items making them very strong in magick and healing energies. These items can be used to store information and such into and will grow as the witch and the circle continues to use it and thus places these positive sacred circle energies into it. Such pieces can also aid in grounding after an intense magickal circle, as it collects any stray positive energy, and eliminates the needed grounding energies for the user to enter the physical plane rejuvenated and clear minded.

3. Colors Of Robes

There are specific colors of robes that are restricted in Wolfen Wicca. Only the High Priestis allowed to wear Black with Gold Trim robes. Only the High Priestess is allowed to wear Purple with Silver

Trim robes. Other than that anything goes! Many (most) practitioners have several robes to wear for many different occasions (Sabbats, Esbats (full moons), sacred occasions, and so on)

4. Stripes on the Sleeves of Robes

Stripes or trim of various color going around the "hem" of the sleeve, closest to the wrist are often used to denote rank in Wolfen Wicca. All are allowed to have 1 stripe of the same color trim as found on the rest of the robe, like the trim usually found on front & hood). However any stripes of color after that are reserved (SEE Fig. 1-4 below)

In our tradition a 1st degree normally shows the regular robe trim all around and 1 extra color (stripe) on sleeve. Each higher rank adds another strip of color to sleeve.

Stripes may not be wider than 1 ½ inches wide after the 1st regular trim. Yes smaller is fine also, but not bigger in this case ☺.

Colors of additional stripes can be any that is chosen by practitioner, as long as it doesn't resemble the High Priest(black with gold) or High Priestess (purple with silver, for many various reasons. Such reasons can include everything from "I like that color' to some great metaphysical reasoning. And yes before you ask, color combinations can vary for each robe you own.

Here's the figures for your reference. The symbols on each shown strip are just there to aid you in identifying between additions of new strip. All strips MUST be a solid color and not patterned or combinations of colors within the strip.

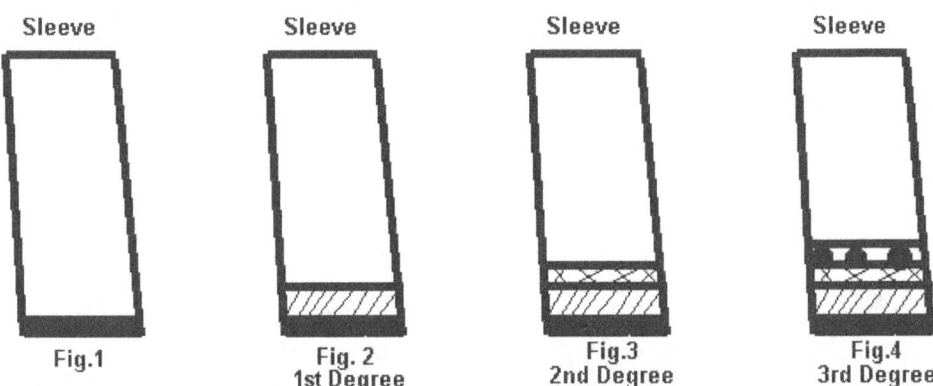

5. Wearing Awards

Many covens and groves give out differing awards of accomplishment and ranks. There are no universal Wiccan Awards and as such these awards will vary from group to group. In Wolfen Wicca awards are usually worn on the Left Breast Side of the role or on the left shoulder, what ever the award deems. Such awards that are worn on the shoulder consist of ropes of specific colors but those are few and far between.

Awards can be worn whenever the practitioner feels like it. They are **expected** to be worn on the 4 High Sabbats and when there are festivals with other groups. Ropes however are always optional as they o tend to get in the way of free movement, yet they do look nice when worn.

Some awards are given in secret achievements and as such are not to be discussed. If asked what the award is for the answer should be something like," Its for exemplary achievements in honoring the Lady & Lord, details of which I cant discuss." Anything more risks permanent loss of the award.

Some awards come with titles. Such titles can be used at anytime the practitioner desires, in full or selected yet they are expected to be announced (used) at the 4 High Sabbats and when there are festivals with other groups. This is usually done at the beginning of the circle when the Circle Caster asks something like; "Who comes to my circle?" Your answer would be your magickal name and titles.

6. Footwear

Footwear is another item that varies from coven/grove to coven/grove (what's new ☺) typically pagan like to feel the Earth below them so shoes are not allowed.

In Wolfen Wicca shoes are not allowed in circles that are meeting inside, out of the weather, yet there are times shoes are allowed. Such times include when meetings outside or when there are long drawn out events outside (where the pavement gets hot enough to cook an egg or mosquitoes make you their number 1

dinner course) for this sandals with socks are ok. Just make sure the shoes are something that's special, magickal and doesn't take away from the magickal setting you are trying to create. White tennis shoes, peeking out from under your robe may cause someone to say "Whats wrong with this picture?"

Yet I also just want to point out that all of these clothing/footwear requirements are just guides, something to work toward. They are not meant in any way to exclude or keep someone from worshiping the God/dess. If you don't have everything all at once that's ok, join in anyway. Just save a little when you can until you reach your goal and you can get the footwear you'd like or the color of material you want or what ever. Don't let these guidelines hold you back, no one is expected to have everything all at once. Heck even at 1 year and a day many people are just finishing everything up they want to acquire.

Bright Blessings,
Forever In The Loving Service Of Others
Lady Wolfen Mists

Class #5
Pre circle Preparation; Personal Sacred Time

© Lady Wolfen Mists Jan.1998

Steps to setting up a Sacred Circle

Wiccans don't usually don't have a special "church like" building we worship in, however this is known to vary from group to group and with weather conditions. Yet traditionally worship is conducted in the wide open expanse of Mother Nature. It can be 'neath a tall oak tree or an open meadow or on a beach, where ever the "heart" of the God/dess lies, this can be a place of worship.

Let's say you found the perfect place you want to do worship/rituals in, what do you need to do next? Well you need to prepare your own personal self/body for worship. You need to remove as many of the negative energies the surround us daily, as you can. How do you do this you ask? Well here are a few recommended ways that are easy to do.

PERSONAL Cleansing Techniques

1. Give yourself at least 1 1/2 hours before you intend to use your circle to get ready. Lay out your special cozy & plush 'sheet' towel and your special soap. I like Sandalwood soap as sandalwood is a purifier and using this soap removes any negative energies you may have collected during the day. Some people use rose soap, as rose is one of the scents related to the Goddess. Any soap will do so long as its "special" to you and ONLY used in your ritual purifying bath, the same goes for the towel.

2. Lay out your favorite music (CD or tape) as well as stick incense and candles if you like. This is to "set the mood" as you soak. It allows you to relax while positive energies from the music flow through you and the smell of your favorite incense signals that the

work day is done, and you are readying for a spiritual experience that evening. A caution however, be sure the music is NOT close to the tub/water while plugged in, don't take any chance it might fall in. we just want to help you relax, NOT Kill you! Also be care where you place the open flames of your candles or incense, we don't want you to catch anything on fire.

3. Another item that I find useful here is crystals set around my tub and the room, Amethysts, Quartz, Rose Quartz and such their energies seem to empower me al the more and aid in my magickal abilities being at their peak.

4. As you fill the tub with water, and you have the music, candles, incense and tapes going, you may now add the traditional cleansing agent....salt! You can use any kind of salt but I like sea salt best as it is more natural. Add about 1/4-1/2 cup of salt per filled salt. Salt has been used for centuries to remove negative energies from the physical and etheric body and prepare them for the reception of positive energies. You can also ass any herbs/bath sachets or bath teas you may wish at this time if you want.

5. Another cleansing agent you can use is Bath Salts that have been prepared for specific purposes. For example lets say you are working on a dream interpretation in your circle ritual for this night. You could use a bit of "Sweetly Comes Your Dreams" bath salts as well as "Purification" Bath Salts to make a powerful combination for the evenings activities. Ok so now you have added whatever cleansing agent you may wish to use. Let the tub fill up with as warm water as you can stand. While it fills take time to brush your hair or stretch your muscles out. Then enter the water and settle back. Saying something aloud like;

> "O beauteous Goddess of Creation
> From who this cleansing water was
> first formed.
> Take the negative thoughts and
> energies from me,
> Make me clean and pure, as this water was,
> in its first seconds of Creation."

Then wash yourself completely and allow yourself time to soak a bit. Next "see" in your minds eye the positive energies/vibrations replacing the negative. As you wash with the sacred soap of your choice, visualize each stroke of the soap gathering these negative energies and throwing them off. At the same time, you will be sealing in the positive energies through the purity of the soap. Meditate to the music and about what you will be doing this night. Now towel off with your special towel. Blow out your incense and candles and put away everything else. Once you feel cleansed and ready you are ready to go get dressed.

6. Before you dress completely take a few minutes to meditate again on what you will be doing and what you wish the outcome to be.

7. Be sure that you have unplugged the tape player, put out the candles, and incense before you leave the house.

What Now?

So now you're cleansed and purified and ready to go. You get in your car and begin your drive to meet others that will worship with you tonight or just on your way to your sacred place. As you are driving every idiot in the city is driving in front of you! Your getting just a bit aggravated! You finally arrive at your destination but the

drive has caused you to draw a few negative energies your way. What to do now, all that work for purity and now.... The answer is easy, and most covens/groves have one of these, a spray bottle full of salt water. You are sprayed lightly as well as the bottom of your bare feet. So all of those "added" energies are released and you are ready to enter the circle again.

What do you carry your items in to the meeting?

You should have a magickal bag that you use to carry only your robe and magickal items in. This bag can be made by you, purchased from us, or even a backpack you pick up for this specific purpose. Remember that any bag you get you can put your own embellishment on making it your bag alone!

I always felt that this bag should be big enough to put your robe in, with another special place for magickal jewelry. It should also be big enough to carry any magickal tools you may want to bring with you, including your Book of Shadows. There should be a pocket on the outside big enough to put your driver's license, checkbook, and keys in, in case you don't want to carry several items. It needs a handle or strap for carrying comfortably. I love my bag its nice to know I have everything in one place when I'm ready to go.

Inside the main place in your bag you should carry a special sachet for purification. This keeps away all the negative energies between home and where your going, affording you a little extra cleansing power to keep the items contained within the bag sacred, purified and holy!

Purification Sachet Recipe   See Practical section on what is needed and how to create this item

Magickal Jewelry Revisited

We have already covered this section however here we will address getting the chosen items ready for circle. In most cases once you have chosen the jewelry you want to wear you will need to clean it. Kinda spiff up its energies, removing any negative ones that may have settled there since last use. An easy cleanser is this purifying water mix. I put some in a spray bottle and carry it in my bag (I use it on tons of stuff not just jewelry)

Energy "Spiffer" Water

    32 oz of Non Tap water (distilled or bottled)

    ½ teaspoon orange peel

    A pinch of salt (Very light pinch)

    2-3 drops of Glycerin

    1-2 drops rose water (or 1 Tablespoon rose petals)

Shake well and spray the water mixture on a tissue or rag and wipe down items. Visualize all the negative energies dissolving and positive energies settling in. Item is ready to use or wear. Spray water is good for about 1-2 weeks, keep in refrigerator when not using.

Different Approaches to Circle Purification

Once you have chosen your actual site of worship the astral place needs cleansings much like your own body. The energies found there may need cleansing as well as a little balancing. This is fairly easy to do and there are several common techniques used.

Salt water can be sprinkled in and around the traditional 9-foot circle, used by solitaries. This cleanses the area and helps to balance the polarities /energies contained within. The salt and water also "erects" the Sacred Sphere that contains the circle. This acts as a barrier to negative energies and prepares your area for sacred worship. It also adds to the reception of positive energies, as well as preparing for any release of energies you may build within your own cone of power.

Another way to cleanse and prepare your sacred space, as the traditional time out of time, and space out of space, is through the use of incense and music. The selection of the incense is important, it should be one that is cleansing, purifying as well as one that invokes the Goddess image within yourself or the God image whatever the case may be. The same goes with the choice of music you wish to use.

Once the music and incense is chosen you are ready for the next step. Let the music play and light the incense. Walk deosil (clock wise) around your circle, letting the incense smoke rise, and visualize

the smoke building the walls of the circle sphere. "See" the smoke chasing or removing any impurities and negative energies and replace them with harmonious balanced energies. Start in the East part of your circle and walk all the way around, meditating for a few seconds at each direction. Return to the East and put out your incense and turn off the music.

If you must leave the circle at this time use the Athame (dagger from the altar or your own private dagger if it differs from the altar one) to "slice" open or unzip a slit that you can step through. Once you have stepped through be sure to "re-zip" the slit to close the opening. This procedure allows for the positive energies to maintain the harmonious balance you created within the circle. If it were to remain open then the energies would "leak out" as well as possible negative energies to "seep" in.

When you are ready to return to use your cleansed space just use the Athame (dagger) to reopen/unzip the slice again. You can cleanse the circle up to 3-5 hours ahead of time if you like.

A FEW OTHER MISCELAINOUS POINTERS

To aid in keeping yourself balanced and in harmony till you get to your circle add a little salt to your shoes.

Sacred Music that you like should be in your bad or car so that you can play it on the way to circle meeting. This aids in focus and meditation putting your mind on notice that you are getting ready to worship.

Just so you know about the proper way to wear your hoods on your robe. They should be up all the time until everyone is in the circle and the circle caster closes the circle from the outside world. It is at this time you enter the astral realm and are in a 'Time out of time and a place out of place." Then the hoods come off, showing the identity of the person. If your coven files out at the end of the circle meeting then as you cross the portal from the circle to mundane Earth then the hoods are put up again hiding the identity of the wearer once more.

One last thing I'd like to cover has to do with hygiene and something a lot of people don't think about in their personal cleansing time. Fresh Breath, Brushed Teeth, and clean smelling feet are a MUST in the circle. So if you naturally have sweaty feet, odor eaters do wonders. For fresh breath be sure to brush before you come and just to make sure that onion covered Taco for lunch isn't still showing up, pop a breath freshener. Cinnamon or cherry candy before entering the circle is nice, both are scents that are sacred, and more than welcome in the presence of the **Lady** and **Lord**.

In the Presence of the Lady

Class #5
Types of incenses

© Lady Wolfen Mists Oct 2000

So what can I tell you about incense? They have been around since tribal times. They usually are made from high quality oils (don't use synthetic here as it smells awful and ruins what your trying to do) Incense also can contain such items as herbs, spices, gums, resins and oils. It is this blending of energies, herbs and oil qualities/attributes, plus the energy you add that aids in the release of a special aroma that raises the vibrational level of those working in the area and of the actual energies being create.

Usually used in rituals to purify the area, to invoke a specific Goddess or God or to perform a special task, like lifting focused energies to the Universe. Incense is a wonderful mood enhancer. It sets up a flow that allows for focused, and concentrated power, in the building of a cone of power within a circle or anywhere it is use. Besides all that they usually smell wonderful.

Incense is often used to represent the element of air and as such is often used in conjunction, but not exclusively, with that direction. Since air can be difficult to symbolize unlike a bowl of Earth for Earth or a glass of water or even hot coals for fire Air is often symbolized by the smoke of incense.

Now there are 4 basic types of incense and thousands of scents for you to choose from when thinking about incense. Different scents can be chosen for various reasons. Such as specific Gods and Goddess's have affinities for certain scents to you want to draw on the natural abilities/qualities of a scent to "I just like it."

Here is a list of the 4 different types of incense
- Stick
- Cone
- Powder
- Granular

Stick and Cone are usually combustible in nature. Meaning that you put a match to them and they catch on fire quickly, burning and then are blown out so that they may smolder. They usually are placed in a burner and allowed to burn at their own rate.

Burners that suite such incense are Banana boat burners like the one shown above or cone burners on which usually have little feet and the cone is sat on a specially heat treated burner and allowed to smolder. These types of incense usually come in a prepackaged pack, ready to go.

Stick and cone incense are nice if you are planning on doing a long meditation and not one will be available to regulate the time or amount of incense to be added at a specific time. They are nice to light in the circle or spell work and just move on to the next item to be addressed in the circle.

The other type of incense is granular and powder incense. These are unusually non-combustible in the since they must be continuously added to a hot charcoal to burn. They are usually home made and work wonderfully.

To use such incense you need 2 special items in addition to the incense itself.
1. A Screen burner
2. Self-igniting Charcoals

Screen Burners are just that burners that come with some type of screen across them on which to sit the charcoal. As The charcoal burns the ashes fall into the 'belly" of the burner and away from the burning charcoal. It sits up to allow for even airflow under the charcoal and keeps the charcoal burning. The only problem with these types of burner is that they get really hot and must be placed on something that protects the surface where its setting so it doesn't scorch.

Now some people say to use a glass ashtray and sit it in a bowl of sand. Then place the charcoal on it. It has been my experience that this just doesn't work well as the glass can crack and break. Now its just simpler for me to pay the $10.00 or so and purchase the item that was made just for this purpose. When dealing with fire its smart not to try and make do, but its up to you.

Self-igniting Charcoals are charcoals that come in rolls usually. They range in size from approx. 1/2 inch to 2 inches. Prices vary but they usually aren't real expensive. These charcoals are lit on one side and then they continue to light themselves. The flame causes the charcoal to 'spit and sputter" as it catches fire and smolders. You can also blow on the charcoal to get it going. These usually burn fairly evenly and are easy to use. Be sure to put it on the screen once it catches fire as it gets hot quickly (yep I'm speaking from experience here). Please DON'T try and use charcoal briquettes to try and save money as they just don't work well and they give off a very unpleasant odor as they burn. Self-igniting charcoals smell a little at first while they catch fire but the odor burns off quickly so you get a clean burn.

So now you have the items you need to burn your granular or powder incense next all you need do is place a small amount on the burning coal. I like granular incense as it allows you more control if the scent and smoke than that of a stick or cone. I can add a pinch here or there in my ritual or spell, as I need. If I need to accentuate an area I add incense, if not I just let it go. Once you add the incense let it burn, if you need to remove some please use a metal spoon for this. On our altar we have the incense we plan to use in a small glass, like a shot glass, all ready to go with a tiny metal spoon (a child spoon) sitting beside the incense ready to use.

To make granular or powdered incense you will need a mortar and pestle in which to grind items to a powder. Also the high quality essential oils I mentioned. Synthetic oils often smell like burning rug or hair so avoid these if you can. Look for high quality granular incense as well as high quality powder. Some powder uses sawdust as a base and then adds oil. Although this looks nice and smells pretty good till you burn it, then it often smokes like crazy and smells like burning wood. The scent of the oils is often over powered by the sawdust base.

  Oh and one more thing, some incense (especially those that are cheaper and made in India) can be nasty when burnt. Now I'm not say all but I have ran across some that the stick is awful and have been dipped in heavy perfume (not oil but perfume, not a good smell burning). They are overpowering in scent but when you burn them they are awful. Some even use animal dung as a base for their incense. So what I'm saying is before you try a new scent in your sacred place give it a try first. Nothing worse than having everyone together and lighting a new incense only to find it gives you a headache and the windows have to be opened to clear the place. Once you find incense you like write it down. I stick with those that I like and have a tendency to stay with that particular line. I trust their quality and feel safe with them.

Bright Blessings,

Forever In The Loving Service Of Others

Lady Wolfen Mists

Class #5

Circle Casting Rite

© Lady Wolfen Mists 07-1992

The circle is considered a very holy, sacred place. Inside many wonderful things happen including spellcasting, worship, healing and communication with the Lady & Lord, just to name a few. The circle should be cast **every time** any form of Magick is to take place.

Before the circle is cast be sure to have purified yourself and the area you intend to use. Then "lay out" the boundaries of your circle. This is done by the circle caster in groups, or yourself if solitary. Traditionally the Athame is used to do this. The caster takes the Athame and walks Deosil (clock wise) beginning in the East.

Invoking

Movement is in a Deosil (clockwise) fashion.

Tools traditionally used are the Athame, however some choose to use the Wand.

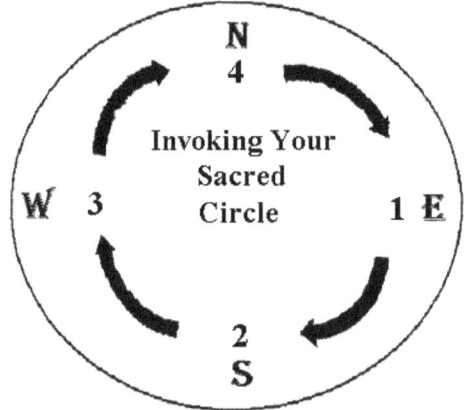

Pointing the Athame at the ground and seeing it making the boundaries of your circle. Once this is completed the caster places

the item back on the altar. When doing this be sure not to close the circle completely, leaving a small section open to pass back and forth through until your ready to begin, if possible allow this section to be the North East section.

Just a side note here; Traditionally the Athame is used to lay down and cast the circle. However I don't like the way it feels and I don't like using it for that purpose. I get a stronger and more intense feeling with the Wand, so I choose to use this. I don't count it against my student to use the Athame or the wand, when working in a circle everything should be as comfortable for you as possible.

Next set up is the Altar. The center is the ideal place for the Altar, facing North or east. Yet if you can't do this then place it where ever it works best for you. Now you may place the tools, cakes and wine upon the altar where they belong. (See Altar Set Up handout) When this has been completed place the candles or markers for the 4 directions (also called the Guardians of the Gates, the Elements, the Watchtowers just to name a few) in the quadrants they will belong. Be sure the candle shave been dressed and made ready for use. Placements of candles are in the following order shown in the table below. These colors may vary from tradition to tradition but these are the most common uses and the ones we use in Wolfen Wicca.

Direction = Element represented	**Color**
East Point---Air	Yellow
South Point---Fire	Red
West Point--- Water	Blue
North Point--- Earth	Green

Bring in all other items you may need for the circle. Set the music, if you are going to use any, cued up and ready to go. Get everyone together for short meditation as they stand waiting to enter the circle. In Wolfen Wicca it is at this time members or sprayed one last time and hoods on robes go up.

The Circle caster enters the circle from the open point and picks up the Athame (or wand) from the altar. The caster then begins to lay down the circle once more. Holding the Athame (or wand) in

both hands, walking deosil (clockwise) once more around the circle. The caster focus their energy through the tool, holding it in both hands with the point down, they see the energy flowing through them and the tool to the floor. This energy makes a circle (actually it's a complete sphere that one creates much like a bubble) and forms the protective boundaries that the group/individual works within.

Once the caster has completed laying the circle out he then goes to the NE corner and faces the people waiting there. The following is said;

Group Circle Caster (GCC);	**"Who comes from the darkness to the light of my circle"?**
Group Response(GR);	"We come to worship and praise the Goddess and God of Light!"
GCC;	**"How do you come?"**
GR;	"In perfect love and perfect trust."
GCC;	**"Then enter in perfect love and perfect trust."**

The circle caster then slices the air with the Athame (or wand) in an up down motion and steps aside. The Group files in. After the group has filed in the caster "zips" p the slice so the energies don't leak out and nothing comes into your sacred site. Next if the caster has used the Athame it is replaced on the altar and the wand is picked up.

The High Priestess and High Priesttake their places in front of the altar. If the grove will be using granular incense for the ritual the Maiden steps forward quietly, usually the first in line and this is done as members file in, and lights the charcoal. Placing the charcoal on the screen burner so it may be ready for use when needed.

    If coven members have brought candles or flashlights into the circle they are extinguished at this point. Hoods remain up.

    The caster lights a taper candle (usually sit up on the right hand corner or the altar, for just this purpose. It is usually small and white.) With the wand in hand the caster moves to the East Gate.

*   I have seen some groups use the Athame for this also but that's up to you. I don't think that inviting spirits or elements to come worship with you looks very friendly with a Dagger/Athame in hand but if your OK with that then that's OK. I have always had much better and friendlier working using the wand, as it seems less threatening than the Athame. However that's the wonderful thing about magick, <u>you do what feels right to you.</u>*

    Now holding the wand in front of you with the hilt down and the point up. The caster faces the East and lights the Yellow candle/light, then says the following, while invoking the pentagram in this direction; (See figure below for Pentagram invocation)

Invoke Pentagram. No circle needed

"And It Harm None..."

Start at #1 and continue till 6. You are standing with your face facing out, projecting the pentagram in front of you.

(c) Lady Wolfen Mists 1996

175

GCC;

> "Guardians, Elementals, Spirits and Sprites of the EAST, we ask that you come forth into our circle. Celebrate with us this time of worship and love. Protect us and aid us in the name of the Lady and Lord of Light!"

Now the caster moves to the South. The caster faces the South and lights the Red candle/light, then says the following, while invoking the pentagram in this direction;

GCC;

> "Guardians, Elementals, Spirits and Sprites of the South, we ask that you come forth into our circle. Celebrate with us this time of worship and love. Protect us and aid us in the name of the Lady and Lord of Light!"

Next the caster moves to the West. The caster faces the West and lights the Blue candle/light, then says the following, while invoking the pentagram in this direction;

GCC;

> "Guardians, Elementals, Spirits and Sprites of the WEST, we ask that you come forth into our circle. Celebrate with us this time of worship and love. Protect us and aid us in the name of the Lady and Lord of Light!"

The next move is to the North. The caster faces the North and lights the Green candle/light, then says the following, while invoking the pentagram in this direction;

GCC;

> "Guardians, Elementals, Spirits and Sprites of the North, we ask that you come forth into our circle. Celebrate with us this time of worship and love. Protect us and aid us in the name of the Lady and Lord of Light!"

(It should be noted that the entire circle turns to face the gate being called. It is also acceptable (even encouraged) for them to add to the power the caster is generating by invoking the pentagram along with the caster at each point.)

With the circle cast and the gates called the caster now returns to the front of the altar and replaces the tool used. The taper is then sat upon the altar, if it has been used to light the gate candle with. The caster now returns to their place with the rest of the members. The High Priestess and High Priestcontinue with the ritual, their hoods are removed. The rest of the members take their hoods off also.

High Priestess:

Facing right side of altar. Lights the white Goddess Candle with taper and says

> "Most Divine Lady, Creatress of all that is, we ask to you join us this evening. That you guide us in our worship, and that you share with us, your children, the hidden mysteries."

High Priest;

Facing the left side of the altar. The High Priestwaits 13 heartbeats before continuing. Reflection at this time by all members on what the joining of the Mother to the group activities will mean to them individually. The taper is picked up once more and the High Priestcontinues;

```
Great Father and most willing Consort, we ask
your presence here this night. In this place
out of time, this place out of space, created
just for you and the Lady's presence. Come Lord
and teach us this night of worship."
```

The High Priest

Continues, he blows upon the charcoal. It should be glowing by now, and sprinkles incense on the charcoal. If you are using stick or cone incense the High Priestlight them now. He says the following;

> "May this sacred incense that rises and floats so high, serve to remind us of the yearning in our souls. That we, too, long to rise above the mundane and become one with the Goddess and God of Light. Breathe deeply of this scent, allow your spirit to take flight and release your souls to the heavens."

All breathe deeply for 13 heartbeats.

The High Priestess;

> "The circle is cast all that have been invited are here. Blessed Be all who stand with us this glorious full moon night!

Group Response;   Blessed BE!

You are now ready to proceed with what ever activities you have scheduled for you circle this night. Your circle is cast!

Protected by Her Loving Light as I find My Way!

Class #5

Banish the Circle Rite

© Lady Wolfen Mists 07-1992

When the ritual is complete the circle MUST be banished, this must be done each and every time a circle is cast. To do this the circle caster takes up the tool once more that the circle was cast with. Begin with the tool that the gates were called with.

Just a quick note on dismissing the Gates. The spirits and sprites of the 4 quarters can sometimes be mischievous and as such you must exercise control over them. When banishing a circle do not be wishy washy in dismissing them. Tell them in no uncertain terms to go and thank them for coming. If you don't you could end up with problems, like a friend of mine.

****

Warning Personal Story about to be told. Skip this part if you don't want to read it.

He was learning to work with the quarters and invoked water to help him in a flowing creativity. He was playing his guitar the phone rang and he went to answer it. He got involved on the phone and went out without dismissing water. When he came home a few hours later there was a water leak in the basement. Luckily his expensive electrical instruments were up high and the water hadn't reached it yet. His sump pump wouldn't click on although he tried and tried. He removed his expensive and heavy I electrical equipment and finally called his landLord to come. The landLord came right away and looked at the mess. The sump pump was new and they couldn't see anything wrong with it.

Finally in desperation the landLord checked the connection. Somehow the connection wasn't complete, although it looked good it had rocked itself out of the wall and want complete so the sump pump want getting the electric current it need to kick on. When it was plugged in it promptly went to work and pumped the basement right out. My friend immediately dismissed the water elements and swears he heard them giggle at the trouble they had cause. He also called me right away to tell e what had happened. So don't be afraid to TELL them what to do without any lead way.

End personal Story Continue ritual

****

Alright so using the tool used to invoke the quarters the caster now uses it once more. This time the caster moves Widdershins (counter clockwise) starting in the North, West, south and ending in East. (see figure below)

Banishment

Movement is in a Widdershins (counter clockwise) fashion.
Tools involved are traditionally the Athame, however some chose to use the Wand.

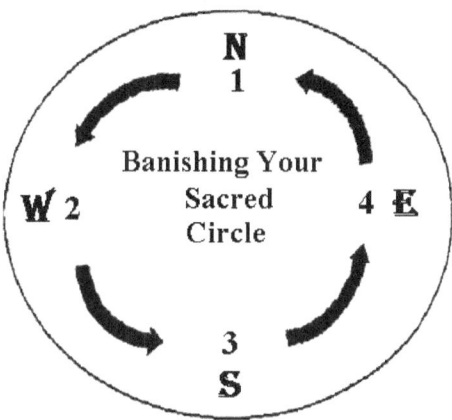

Grove members turn to each direction once more and may add their energies to the banishment by using the banishment pentagram at each quarter. You don't need to add the circle around the pentagram unless you want. Another its up to you thing.

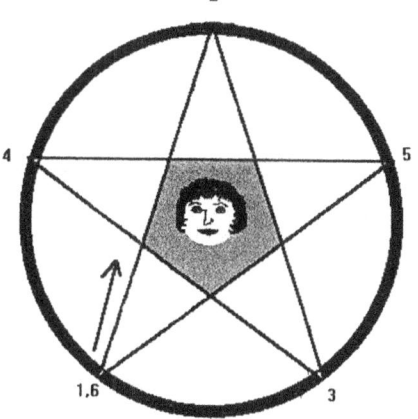

Banish Pentagram, No circle needed

"Do What Ye Will....."
Start a #1 and continue till 6. You are standing with your face facing out, projecting the pentagram in front of you.

(c) Lady Wolfen Mists 1996

At each direction the tool is held the same way as when it was cast. The banishment pentagram is used.

Grove Circle Caster; "Guardians, Elementals, Spirits and Sprites of the NORTH. We thank you for your presence here at this time of worship. Yet now comes the time for you to return to your homes. Leave only your love and protection to keep us safe. Until next time we gather and meet. Merry we part!"

The GREEN Candle is snuffed out. The Caster moves to the next quarter.

Grove Circle Caster; "Guardians, Elementals, Spirits and Sprites of the WEST. We thank you for your presence here at this time of worship. Yet now comes the time for you to return to your homes. Leave only your love and protection to keep us safe. Until next time we gather and meet. Merry we part!"

The BLUE Candle is snuffed out. The Caster moves to the next quarter.

Grove Circle Caster; "Guardians, Elementals, Spirits and Sprites of the SOUTH. We thank you for your presence here at this time of worship. Yet now comes the time for you to return to your homes. Leave only your love and protection to keep us safe. Until next time we gather and meet. Merry we part!"

The RED Candle is snuffed out. The Caster moves to the next quarter.

Grove Circle Caster;   "Guardians, Elementals, Spirits and Sprites of the EAST. We thank you for your presence here at this time of worship. Yet now comes the time for you to return to your homes. Leave only your love and protection to keep us safe. Until next time we gather and meet. Merry we part!"

The YELLOW Candle is snuffed out. The Caster moves to the next quarter.

When all the directions have been thanked and sent home, the caster returns the tool to the altar. The caster returns to the rest of the circle. The High Priestess and High Priestsay the following together or share different lines.

High Priestess & High Priest;

"Mother of Love and Beauty **Father of Justice and stability, We wish to take this time to thank you all for your**
mercies and guidance. We must end and
banish this time out of time and this place out
of place. Yet we beg and beseech you both to
continue to watch us and guides us. Lift us up
when we have need and stay by our sides so
that we never walk alone.

Mother we swear that we shall never forget those who trod the road before us. That we will do our best to represent you with honor and wisdom.

Father, continue to protect us until we meet again. Keep us upon the path of Light and in a mind where Harm Ye None is first and foremost.

<u>**High Priest/ess**</u>

<u>**Both say**</u>

This circle is closed this right is ended! Merry we part!

All Gove say;   "Blessed Be!"

<u>**High Priest/ess**</u>

<u>**Both say**</u>

"So Mote It Be!"

The candles are snuffed out all is in darkness.

Lights are then put back on and clean up by Maiden and Grove Tender. Tools are cleaned and stored by circle caster. Robes are stored. Food from cakes and wine are placed outside.

Class #5
Invoke -Banish Circle Handout
Quick reference

© Lady Wolfen Mists 07-1992

Invoking

Movement is in a Deosil (clockwise) fashion.
Tools traditionally used are the Athame, however some choose to use the Wand.

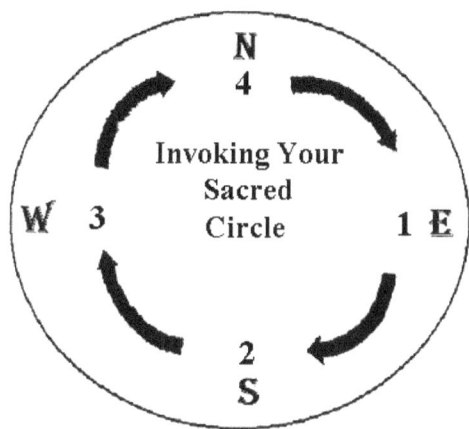

Banishment

Movement is in a Widdershins (counter clockwise) fashion.
Tools involved are traditionally the Athame, however some chose to use the Wand.

Class #5
Invoke & Banish Pentagram Handout for circles

© Lady Wolfen Mists 07-1992

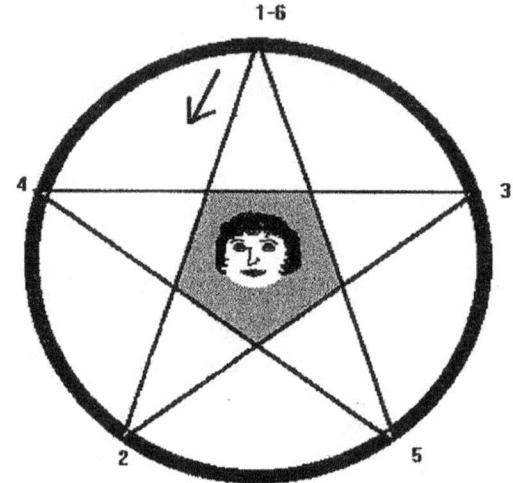

Invoke Pentagram, No circle needed

"And It Harm None..."

Start a #1 and continue till 6. You are standing with your face facing out, projecting the pentagram in front of you.

(c) Lady Wolfen Mists 1996

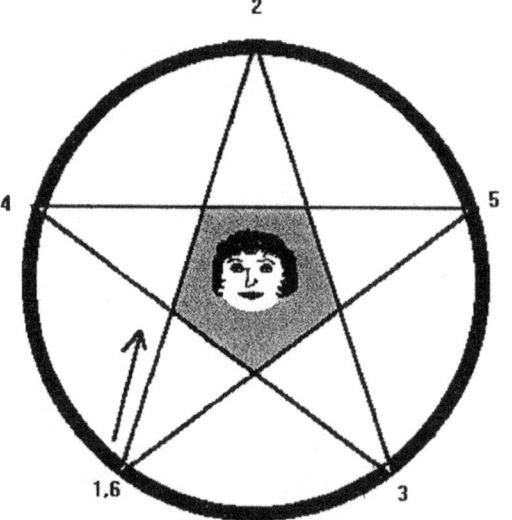

Banish Pentagram, No circle needed

"Do What Ye Will....."

Start a #1 and continue till 6. You are standing with your face facing out, projecting the pentagram in front of you.

(c) Lady Wolfen Mists 1996

Class #5
Altar Set Up Handout

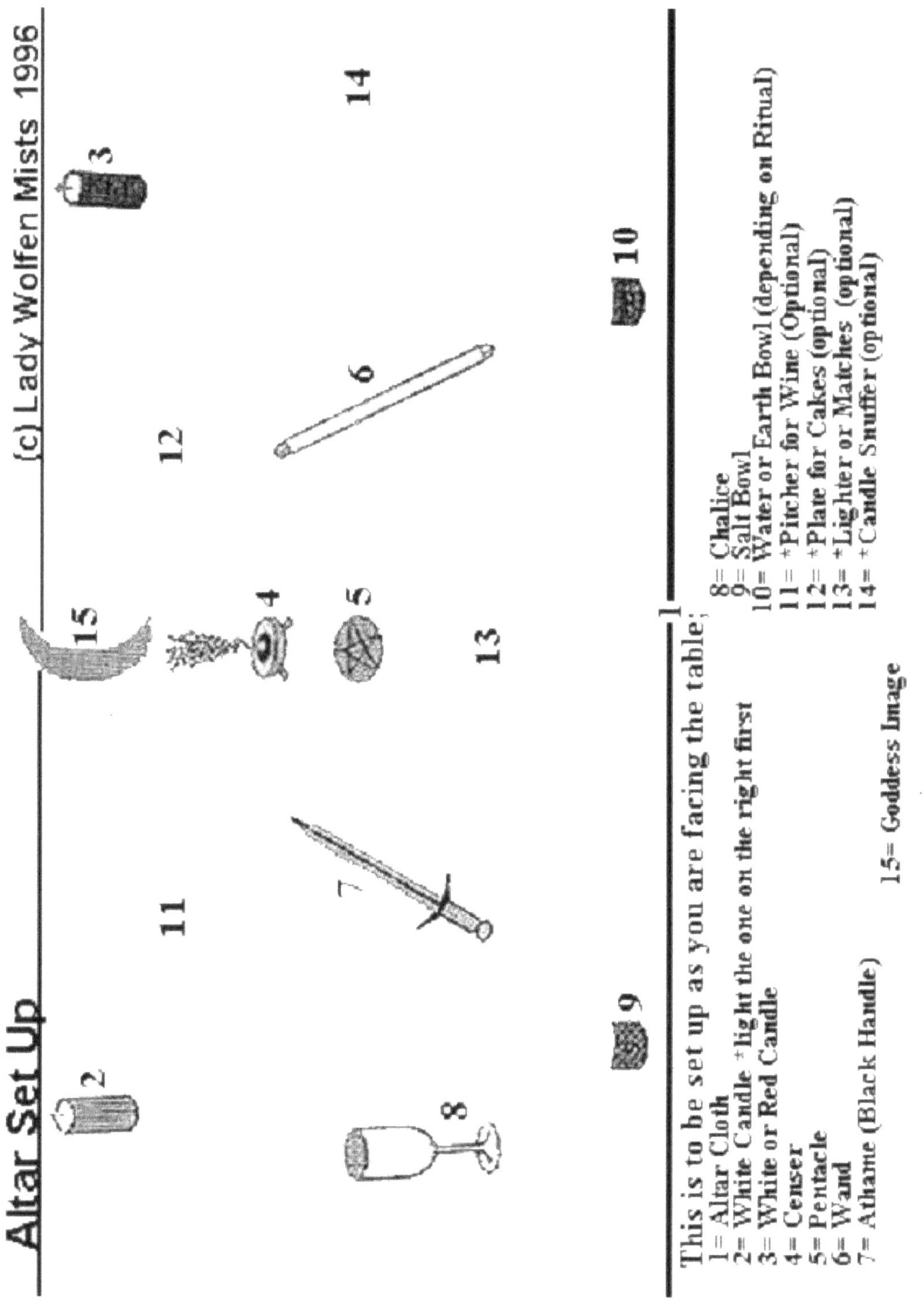

Altar Set Up

(c) Lady Wolfen Mists 1996

This is to be set up as you are facing the table;

1= Altar Cloth
2= White Candle *light the one on the right first
3= White or Red Candle
4= Censer
5= Pentacle
6= Wand
7= Athame (Black Handle)
8= Chalice
9= Salt Bowl
10= Water or Earth Bowl (depending on Ritual)
11= *Pitcher for Wine (Optional)
12= *Plate for Cakes (optional)
13= *Lighter or Matches (optional)
14= *Candle Snuffer (optional)
15= Goddess Image

Class #5

Cakes and Wine

© Lady Wolfen Mists 07-1992

Cakes and wine is a very sacred part of the circle ritual. It is the representation of the energies of the Goddess and God and how they feed us not only on the physical level but on the spiritual level also. How the Goddess feeds us from her body (manifested as food and libations on this Earth plane) and how such food is the renewal of our own wheel of life. It should be done with much humility and reverence at each and every full moon (Esbat) and Sabbat gathering.

There should be enough cakes (we use cookies in moon shapes or such) for each member to have one and one each extra to represent the Goddess and God. We also put one in for any missing members who may be ill and often send them home with someone to give the person so they may join in also.

Here is the ritual we use, it is simple and easy to follow, yet it is charged with energy and emotion.

The High Priestess holds the Cakes in her left hand, with her right hand poised over the plate. She focuses positive energies and releases them into the cakes.

High Priestess:

"As it was done on the ancient hills by bonfires,

As it was done by shadows and moonlight.

As it was done by those who paved our way,

So we do today in the same spirit. We ask for Blessings of Life.

These cakes, who's meal grew from the earth, sustain us in life and combines with our bodies. Thus in the end, like all things, returns to the Earth. To once again be renewed.

This is the way of the Ancients, The never ending cycle of Birth, Life, Death and Re-birth! May we think on those ancient mysteries and wipe away the veil of mystery, gaining understanding and wisdom, as we par take of these cakes. Blessed be!

All say; "Blessed Be!"

The High Priesttakes a Cake and gives it to the High Priestess, She in turn serves him.

Then the Maiden or Grove Tender come up and takes the plate to serve the other members of the coven. Each person takes a cake and holds it. The extra cakes are placed back upon the altar.

The High Priestthen takes up the Chalice. This is where it can get tricky. Now in the old days most people drank directly from the chalice as it was passed from member to member, but to day with thought of hygiene and such we prefer to use individual cups. As such a pitcher of liquid is sat aside with enough cups for each member to have one. The chalice on the altar is filled and this is the cup that is blessed or you can bless the pitcher directly.

What I like to do is bless the chalice and pour some of that into the already filled awaiting pitcher, then fill the cups from there. The liquid is still high in energies and half is left on the altar for the Bright Lady and Lord. In Wolfen Wicca we do not use alcoholic beverages in the circle, in respect for those in recovery. Instead we use sparkling cider, soda, even juice or sparkling water and so on. Ok enough said now on with the ritual.

The High Priesttakes up the chalice in his left hand and with his right poised over it says the following;

High Priest;

" In this cup flows the life blood of the Earth. It was given and taken by those who walk the way of the wise, in eons past. It is shared with those of us who choose that same path today. In perfect Love and Trust grow these precious buds of life. As we sip and drink from the blessed fountain, May our thirst be quenched. May ours souls be stilled. May we strive to satisfy our thirst in Their house of Light forever. Blessed Be!

All say;   "Blessed Be!"

The High Priestess holds the pitcher forward and the High Priestpours half of the Blessed Liquid into the waiting to serve pitcher.

cups)

The Grove Tender or Maiden set out the cups (we use small paper and begin pouring the Liquid, The High Priestand Priestess are served first. The Grove Tender serves everyone else. The cakes are eaten and the liquid is drunk, meditation for a few minutes is allowed.

The circle is usually opened at this point and people share grips, wants, thanks, stories of blessings, pats on the backs, announcements and anything they want to share.

When sharing is completed the High Priestess closes the circle and the Grove tender collects the cups and the ceremony continues to the next scheduled event.

End cakes and wine ceremony

Class #5
Make a Purification Sachet

© Lady Wolfen Mists 07-1990

Below is the recipe for the Purification Sachet, and the ingredients to make it. Remember that a part is any equal measure you want it to be. It can be a teaspoon to a cup just make sure the parts are the same through out the recipe. Here a part is equal to a tablespoon.

Purification Sachet Recipe   1 part = 1 tablespoon approx.

- 1 small muslin/cotton bag
- 1 pinch of Sandalwood
- 2 parts Sage
- 1 part Frankincense Tears (optional)
- 1 part Cinnamon
- 2 parts Rose petals
- 1 part Lavender
- 1 part Angel wings (optional)
- 1 small Black Obsidian stone or Red Jasper or both

Mix items well in a bowl going in a deosil direction well. As you mix in each item "see," in your minds eye, the cleansing abilities of this purification item grow. "See" all the dark and black negativity leave the body, leaving it clean and lightfilled. Finally add the stones and allow all to sit for the count of 13 heartbeats. Next put the mixture into the cotton/muslin bag tie closed.

In the tub or shower hang it over the water faucet allowing the water to run through it and in turn over you. As it flows over you it will cleanse away the unwanted misaligned energies and you are fresh and cleansed and ready for the circle.

    This can be used again and again. When you feel it is losing its cleansing energy just whip up a new batch and throw the old used mixture out. Its simple, easy and really works!

Class #5
Test What You Have learned

© Lady Wolfen Mists 2000

Do a circle casting write in your Grimoire how it went

1. Skyclad is someone who's

　　__(A) Dressed in blue for the circle 　　__(C) Naked in the circle

　　__(B) Mind is in the clouds 　　__(D) Dressed in a robe of White

True or False (with reference to Wolfen Wicca)

2. _____ 1st Degree Initiates can wear crowns in the circle

3. _____ Only the High Priestcan wear Amber & Jet in the circle

4. _____ Salt is considered the traditional cleansing tool.

5. _____ It's not necessary to take special time for cleansing before coming to circle.

6. Name the different types of Incense discussed.

7. Explain how the above incense is used.

8. Why do we create sacred circle spaces?

9. What are the 4 directions & corresponding colors & elements

10. Write a short paragraph on your circle casting and how it went.

Wolfen Wicca ®
Class #6

© Lady Wolfen Mists Jan.1990

revised 2000

Class #6

Theory;

Spirit Guides (types)

Summerland

Soul Sending Rite

Funeral herbs

Traditional Sabbat Herbs

Dangerous Herbs for Pregnant Woman

Talking Spirit Boards

Practical;

Do Soul Sending Rite write in your Grimore about it

Test

Class #6

Spirit Guides

© Lady Wolfen Mists 1996

Every one has a spirit guide. Some of us are more "in tune" with our inner self than others so we are more aware of them. But rest assured even if you have never met your spirit Guide it's been there all along. Guiding you in subtle ways, helping you and teaching you. With the help of these Spirit Guides we can experience the emotional, physical and spiritual lessons of this life with the help of someone or something that cares for us and who truly has our best interest at heart. Through this interchange and interaction we are able to improve and enrich the insight we gain from the karmic lessons, struggles and ordeals that become parts of our everyday lives. These Spirit Guides help us see how such experiences can be elevated beyond the physical and examined as a spiritual message.

There are many types of Spirit Guides for many many various reasons, but for now we will look a 5 basic types.

Spirit Helpers

The first I like to call Spirit Helpers. These are usually animals, much like power animals in shamanism. There are usually three (3) basic animals at a time that are a part of you, that aid in making up who you are at that very moment in time. Now there can be more but I have found that there are at least 3 that are yours especially.

Let me explain further. There can be such animals as a bear in your personality make up. Bear is there to teach you introspection's as well as assertive qualities and protectiveness. Maybe Otter is found in your make up also, otter teaches feminine traits and fun. Then maybe horse follows.

Horse is raw power! Power of creation and of putting into manifestation all the ideas you have. These animals help make up who you are at that moment and can be called upon to aid you in accessing their characteristics and qualities. They help you understand and come into balance with all around you. These

animals may reside at your safe place, they can not be owned they simply come to you because of a need and you should be greatly honored that they choose to work with you not for you. There is much to learn from spirit helpers, listen and learn.

Now Spirit Helpers stay for as long as they deem the need to be, then another may take their place. Some stay a lifetime or many life times while others just visit for a stage in your journey. All may be accessed and talked to in your safe place at any time.

Before you ask, such animals I speak of here do not have to be Earth reality based. Yes you can have Dragons, Griffins & Unicorns and others of which the likes we do not know. In any case they are a real part of you and as such deserve your respect and your acknowledgment and your thanks.

Guides who you knew on Earth plane

The second Type of spirit guides are Earth Based Spirits who have crossed. This can be anyone from a relative to the Old lady down the street to a friend but they are someone you knew in this lifetime. Someone who was active in your life and who aided you. That person you could always call on for help and they would answer. They are still active in your life after they "cross" and still try to guide you and help you in any way they can.

Guides from a Past Life

The third type are people from past lives. They are usually from your soul group, meaning that you have spent many lives together incarnating often at the same time. They are at the same level of spiritual advancement as you are and are "soul friends."

They are there to aid you in "getting" your lessons so you can continue to spiritually advance. They are usually intertwined in helping you get through all the past life karmic issues (both positive and negative, remember Karma isn't just bad.) They guide you in realizing the gifts and talents you have stored away from achievements in past lives.

They pretty much aid you seeing the full essence of the self and in growing and adding to the aspect of who and what you truly are, for that is their main job...to help you grow and reach higher spiritual levels.

<u>Guides from a Other Planes and Dimensions</u>

The fourth type of spirit Guide is often misunderstood. They are beings that are not from our time or place. They can be from other planets or even other dimensions. The problem with many of these beings is that they do not look like anything we have ever seen before so they scare us. We think of them as monsters and such.

Remember when you were a child and you used to see "boogie men" at night, maybe coming out of the closet. No one ever believed you but you know they were real and they were there at the foot of your bed. You were drawn to these spirits, but at the same time there was fear and panic associated with them, cause they came to you at night when you were alone.

Such beings may have been spirit guides from other places. Why did they come to a child? Because a child is open and sees many things that we as adults have been socially programmed not to see. They came to make contact with you, but upon realizing the fear you associate with them they ceased to "show" themselves to you. But don't take that to mean they don't still interact with you on a more spiritual level. They are ready to make themselves known to you when you can accept them without such fear. So don't be astounded if you meet your spirit guide and it resembles a childhood "monster" it has been there many years looking out for you and helping you succeed.

Just a quick personal note; It has been my experience (and the same for many of my students) that many healers see and remember such visitors from child hood. Then upon meeting some of their healing guides they are face to face with them once more. These advanced beings from other planes and dimensions have much knowledge to share, especially healing knowledge and are kind, loving and compassionate despite their appearance. The key here to seeing

if this is a gentle being is your intuition, if once in its presence you feel "icky" then follow that and leave. If however as many report, after getting through the initial shock of the appearance they feel warm and loving light from the guide then you know this is a caring being who has your best interest at heart.

Master Guides

The final Spirit Guides we will take a look at is considered Master Guides. These are guides that are assigned to special people who are destined to be Spiritual Leaders, or Avatars. This master guide is several spiritual planes above you and helps you learn to lead. They guide you in making the best possible decisions, grant wisdom when needed and instills a respectable ethical standard in your very soul. They aid you in making you a clear connection to the Goddess and God and help you to receive clear messages from them. They also hold classes on the astral/dreamtime where you attend and teach you many of the great mysteries spiritual leaders need to know. They teach you how to 'give ' this information to others in the best possible way and aid you in the accession process of your own spiritual well being and evolution. It is an awesome task to be a spiritual Leader and not for everyone, these guides make such a task easier.

Class #6

Summerland

© Lady Wolfen Mists 1996

One question that everyone asks is, if there is no heaven or hell where do you go when you die? In Wolfen Wicca ™, we call the place you go to the Summerland. It is known by many other names as well by other traditions such as, Land of the Faerie, the Shining Land, or the Land of the Young. It is not considered a physical material place, it is considered to be more of a spiritual gathering place in the presence of the God and Goddess.

It is a place that everyone from Mother Theresa to Hitler goes to. It is a place of rest and relaxation to abide with the God and Goddess and our soul group until it is time to reincarnate to learn another lesson. It is that site where we return from life, so that we may continue the never- ending cycle of birth, life, death and re-birth.

I explain it much like this; the Summerland is much like a bus terminal where everyone must pass through to get to where ever they are planning to go in the long run. It is a stop in your spiritual evolution. It makes no judgments on you, it is simply there for you to have a place to rest and relax until your next lesson starts.

When you die (I like cross better for the word die sounds so final and crossing is far from final) you are escorted to the Summerland by the God, He presents you to the Lady. There is much rejoicing at your return and many friends (both human and non) and soul group members look forward to reconnecting and visiting with.

But first things first with your arrival. You go with the Lady and Lord to a separate place it is here your last life incarnation contract (for lack of a better word) is pulled up. Together you then review your entire life, yep that's everything you ever did. You look at the contract you made.

For example in this lifetime you agree to learn the lesson of compassion. The Lady and Lord put opportunities for you to learn this lesson in your life experience. If you get it right off then you move to another agreed upon lesson, if not the lesson is repeated over and over (in a stronger and stronger way) so you have every chance to "get it." That is the reason for many peoples cycles in their lives, they just aren't getting the lesson they need to learn so it keeps popping up till they do get it. If they don't get it this lifetime they just give it a shot in yet another, but the lesson remains very strong and grows stronger each time it must be repeated.

But back to the Compassion lesson. Ok so you contract to learn compassion, in your life review you see a time you were really in a big hurry, late for a meeting. On the curb sat a person who looked homeless, tired, cold and hungry. They were crying! Did you stop and ask them if you could help? Did you take the time to feed them and reach out to their soul, did you see that they were warmed. Did you realize that but for the love of the Goddess and God that could be you sitting they're alone, dirty and hungry? Or did you simply walk around them and on your way to your meeting, maybe even thinking that the streets are getting full of these people? Yet another time did you ignore the needs of a neighbor who was lonely cause you were to busy? All they ask for was a little time, maybe a cup coffee, some conversation and a warm smile. Where was your compassion? It is you who decides how well you did, not the Lady and Lord.

It is you who figures out, with brutal honesty, if you needed to try and learn that lesson again. No one but you is responsible, not destiny, not the God and Goddess you are solely responsible for your own spiritual well being and the advancement of your soul and the lessons you choose to learn or not learn. Once you have concluded how well you did in this lifetime you sit with the Goddess and God and talk about all that you did learn, all your experiences, all the feelings you had while living there. Yes I know this sound overwhelming but that's how we believe it works. Kinda puts a new meaning to the words responsibility doesn't it. You decide how you did and the God and Goddess decide what spiritual advancement level you are at. At this time you may also make a new contract on what it is you would like to learn in your next incarnation or you can wait.

Then after the life review you go out to explore the Summerland. There will be people you know there waiting to see you, much feasting and merriment go one. You can stay as long as you like, and enjoy as much as you want. You are the one who decides when you incarnate again and if it will be on this Earth plane or another, you are the one who decides the lesson to attempt to learn in your re-incarnation.

What does the Summerland look like

Like most things in magick every Wiccan has their own description of the Summerland. Some see it as very mystical with great standing stones and pristine plants and rivers everywhere. Others see it as a jungle, while still others see it as space, maybe filled with whirling energies and stars and planets. Just about everyone agrees that all life forms (human and non) can connect here and come into the presence of the Divine Lady and Her Consort, the Lord.

So as you can see I can't give you a cut and dried answer here, its your magick and as such it must be your vision of the Summerland you follow. Although in Wolfen Wicca ® we do have some beliefs in common, like the life review, seeing the Lady and Lord, and reuniting with friends for as long as we wish until our rebirth.

I know what I believe the Summerland to look like but that is my vision. I still like to make the magick system somewhat your own, giving you room to adjust it to fit you, this is a highly personal religion and as such you must reflect what works for you, after all you are the expert on your own magick. So I leave the Summerland description like this, basically the Summerland is anything you want it to be.

Class #6
Soul Sending Rite for the Solitary Practitioner

© Lady Wolfen Mists Jan.1998

This rite has been used many times, from people that have crossed to animals, it has always helped me to heal and to honor those that have crossed.

Soul Sending Rite for the Solitary Practitioner

© Lady Wolfen Mists © 07-01-1992 revised 1998

I, Lady Wolfen Mists, wrote this rite. It is to aid those who have crossed that you wish to do something special for. Perhaps you didn't get to the memorial, or funeral, or you didn't get to say goodbye in a comfortable pagan way. This rite is aimed at that, as well as aiding you in healing.

Many have used it and say it aided them in to many ways to count. I give it to you here freely, all I ask is that you not change it too much and give me credit for it. Although this rite is aimed at the solitary practitioner but can easily be adjusted to fit groups. Blessings

This rite should be done only after candles are "dressed," and circle is cast or area is purified. This ritual is to be done to aid in sending someone to the Summerland. Full moon is best, but any moon phase will work.

This rite can be done as soon as someone crosses, or years later when you feel that you are ready to release that spirit. It can also be done if you have just found out that someone has crossed (no matter how long the time of the actual crossing has been compared to the time you find out), or if you simply were unable to make it to the funeral. This rite aids you in the healing of a loss, it is meant to help you say the things you never got to say and "know" that they will hear you and in many cases speak back to you.

You will need:

    1 pack Matches

    2--White Taper candles

    1--Taper candle of their favorite color

    Incense--I recommend Spirit or Sandalwood for stick incense, for granular try Friendship or Astral, yet in all honesty anything pleasing to you will work

    *Something of theirs if possible or something to symbolize them

    * Something special to symbolize the Goddess

You will first set up a small altar, with two white candles in the back positioned one each corner side by side. In front of the candles you will place the incense burner. On the left side you will place your symbol of the Goddess. On the right side you will place the candle of their favorite color, then in front of it all place the persons personal item or the item that symbolizes them.

See below for Altar set up:

    White Candle..White Candle

                            Incense Burner

    Goddess Symbol,..Candle for person who crossed,

    ....Persons personal item...........................
    .... Or item to symbolize them........................

Once this is set up do the following, light the two white candles saying;

"Lord and Lady of Light, I, <u>your name</u>, now humbly come into your presence."

Now light the incense, as it burns walk deosil (clock-wise) around the circle, saying:

"Mother of All, Creatress. Father of Life, Bringer of Death
Undines, Fire Elementals, Fairies and Sprites,
Heed the words of a Child of the Light.
I come before you to ask that you aid the way of one who has crossed over.
Make, <u>person's name</u>, transition to the next level safe, easy, and pain free."

Next light the candle of their favorite color, saying the following:

"The name of the one who has walked through the veil and journeyed on that ancient path is,
<u>their full name.</u>
They were and are my,*(identify their role as many as you wish to honor, i.e. friend, heart brother or sister and so on)*"

Now take the time to tell the Lady and Lord about the person who has crossed over. Talk about your memories both good and bad; speak of how they influenced your life and the bonds that you made together. It's ok to become very emotional at this time, pour your heart out. Say all that fills your heart. Tell the Lord and Lady why you wish them to especially look out over this loved one. Once you have finished and your heart feels lighter, you are ready to move on.

Pick up the candle of their favorite color and place it on the left side of the altar, along side the Goddess symbol. Take a few minutes

(about 13 heartbeats) and say the following;

"Goddess I pray that you place, <u>their name</u>, into the hands of the Father.

That they may dwell with Him until they are reborn and renewed.

That they may seek out Your wisdom and dwell in Your Unconditional Loving Light.

I pray that the eternal cycle continue. That, <u>their name</u>, ascends to those planes, that may be needed to complete his/her souls development.

Send them my eternal love and caring.

May Your love aid us both in meeting again in the Summerland, whence comes my time to walk the long path.

I ask of the Mother to cleanse my heart of the pain of this loss, after I have mourned my loss of a physical connection and grieved, as I may need.

I ask that She help me to remember that the Circle of Life, Death, and Rebirth continues.

I ask the Father to aid me in learning the lessons of Love on all levels and of Life at this painful time.

I implore Him to teach me strength, that I may meet my passing with dignity and acceptance and understanding.

Strength I beseech of thee both, at this time to aid me to continue to grow and face life in a loving and spirited way, even though, <u>their name</u> is no longer physically here to share this with me.

Yet let me be content in the knowledge that on the higher spiritual plane

<u>their name</u> **grows and thrives.**

May I rest knowing that there is no final end to that part of us, that very best part of us, that holds our true essence of life!"

While their candle continues to burn, sit and visualize them stepping up to a beautiful portal and turning to speak with you. "See" their astral essence moving on to all the etheric levels, as we are all meant to do. If need be for yourself you can communicate with them at this time. Tell them all you need to say, and LISTEN to what they may tell you. Wish them Perfect Love and Perfect Trust. Tell them that you release their spirit and will not hold them back, bound to this earthly plane by your need to keep them here with you. Then Kiss them or hug them, and allow them to enter the lighted gate that opens to the Summerland.

Upon completing your visualization, if their candle is still burning, allow it to burn a bit longer then put it out.

Say the following after the candle is out;

"All that has gone on here tonight for: <u>*Your Full Name*</u> and <u>*Their Full Name*</u>, was done in love, trust, respect and honor.

Thank you Goddess and God for your intercession and understanding.

I release any ties I have that may bind this spirit to this physical world.

I look forward to our seeing each other again when I too am called home.

As it has been done,

So Mote It Be!"

****

Banish your circle, if you cast a complete circle. If the candles are still burning snuff them out, put out your incense. Clean up and put away your items. You may wish to store your items in a special box for memories or you can get rid of them, what ever feels right to you. Your Soul Sending rite is done.

Blessings and healings to you all,
Lady Wolfen Mists

Class #6
Traditional herbs used in funerals

Someone you know has died; you want to honor them but are unsure what to do. Maybe you want to do something private, not drawing a lot of attention to the act, but you don't know what. How about carrying some Rosemary on you during the funeral procession, or placing some oak pieces in the coffin or at the grave for renewal of the soul or to finish any unfinished business you may have had with them.

The following is a list of herbs that have been traditionally used to honor and aid the Crossing Over of living beings. They can be used as incense at the funeral, as well as salting the grave site, or the home of the being that has crossed. Other uses include wearing the scents in honor of the dead, or as decorations in burial places or homes of the living who are grieving.

BASIL: Protection, Love

BAY LAUREL: - Communicating with the dead, protection, triumph, A must for funeral wreaths.

BIRCH: Rebirth. Renewal

CEDAR: Prosperity, Purification.

COMFREY: Healing.

CYPRESS: Endings. Karma cycles are over

ELDER: Transformation

FRANKINCENSE: Purification, Spiritual Transformation.

GARLIC: Protection for negative energies

HOLLY: Renewal, Resurrection.

IVY: Rebirth, Celebration.

LAVENDER: Memories, Peace.

LEMON BALM: - Immortality, happiness; used in a tea for emotional cleansing and uplifting.

LILY: Resurrection.

MINT: Joy, Good in tea to bring restful sleep for the grieving

MISTLETOE: Protection.

MUGWORT: Inner Sight

MULLEN: Cleansing.

MYRRH: Healing, Purification, Protection, Used in Mummifying.

OAK: Strength. Renewal of the soul, healing of wounds (unfinished business)

PARSLEY: - Good luck in here after; decorating tombs, altars to the dead

PERIWINKLE: Immortality, " Flower of the Dead, " Placed on graves.

POMEGRANATE: Rebirth.

POPPY: Restfulness.

ROSEMARY: - Friendship, purification, happiness; tossed into open graves " for remembrance, " burned as incense, carried in funeral processions, to aid the dead in finding their way.

ROSES: Love Purification.

ROWAN WOOD AND BERRIES: Protection.

RUE: Karmic Completion.

SAGE: Wisdom, Purification.

SANDLWOOD: Purification.

THYME: Purification.

WILLOW: Releases, Cleansing.

WORMWOOD: Transformation.

YARROW: Protection, Healing.

YEW: Immortality, endings; once planted in graveyards to protect bodies of the departed.

******It should be noted that this list is to be Credited to **Selana Fox**, it was given to me by a friend, I hope you find it as useful as I have. Thanks for all the great work you have done for the pagan community Selana****

Class #6
Herbs for Sabbats

© Lady Wolfen Mists Jan. 1998

This list is given to you so that you can have a quick reference of herbs that are traditionally used for Sabbats. It is not intended to be exhaustive in nature, as entire books have been written on this subject, its just a handy reference guide to the more common herbs you can easily find.

In many Sabbats there is a time for the remembrance of one who has crossed. This list is to aid you in finding the proper herb to empower and enhance your energies. It can be used along with other herbs to aid I honoring and remembering those who have crossed, both human and non.

I must also put a caution here on the herbs included on this list some may not be for ingestion as they could be poisonous. Please be sure to check with a competent source before burning or ingesting such herbs. For example Tansy may be ok for most of us but it can cause miscarriage in pregnant women. I suggest you get a good reference book for your herbal work. Any of the herb books by Scott Cunningham is excellent!

Sabbat Herbs

SAMHAIN	Apple, Broom, Dittany of Crete, Mandrake, Mint, Mullein, Nutmeg, Oak, Sage, Wormwood.
YULE	Ash, Bay, Cedar, Chamomile, Frankincense, Ivy, Juniper, Mistletoe, Oak, Pine, Rosemary, Sage, Sandalwood
IMBOLC	Angelica, Basil, Bay, Benzoin, Blackberry, Cinnamon, Coltsfoot, Frankincense, Mace, Myrrh, Violet.
OSTARA	Broom, Cinquefoil, Dogwood, Jasmine, Lavender, Peony, Rose, Strawberry, Tansy
BELTANE	Almond, Apple, Ash, Calendula, Clover, Frankincense, Hawthorn, Ivy, Lilac, Rose, Rowan
MIDSUMMER	Basil, Wood Betony, Chamomile, Dogwood, Elder, Fennel, Fern, Frankincense, Lavender, Lemon, Mugwort, St.John's Wort, Vervain.
MABON	Balm of Gilead, Benzoin, Calendula, Cypress, Fern, Myrrh, Oak, Pine, Rose, Sage, Thistle.
LUGHNASSADH	Acacia, Blackberry, Frankincense, Mistletoe, Oak, Rose, Sandalwood.

Class #6

Known Dangerous Herbs for Pregnant Woman

© Compiled by Lady Wolfen Mists 1999

Here's a list that I have complied of **Herbs** that are **KNOWN to be dangerous to Pregnant Women,** it is not exhaustive (I'm sure there are many more out there) its just a few for my personal reference. Ones that are more common.

HERB   **Danger**

Herb	Danger
Angelica;	Has **sterols & saponins**. These are in doses that far exceed the safety factor for pregnancy.
Blackberry Tea And Raspberry Tea;	**DO NOT** drink or ingest during early pregnancy, acts as a uterine stimulant.
Black Cohosh...(also Blue Cohosh);	**AVIOD** Can cause miscarriage
Burdock;	**AVIOD** Can cause miscarriage
Chamomile;	Avoid in **ALL its forms**! This includes the "herbal teas" *Use Caution:* MAY CAUSE MISCARRIAGE!!
Cinnamon Oil;	*Use Caution:* MAY CAUSE MISCARRIAGE!
Cow Parsnip (Yerba del Oso);	Has **sterols & saponins**. These are in doses that far exceed the safety factor for pregnancy
Hyssop;	*Use Caution* MAY POSSIBLY CAUSE MISCARRIAGE!!
Immortal;	*Use Caution:* MAY POSSIBLY CAUSE MISCARRIAGE!!
Mistletoe;	**VERY DANGEROUS: DEFINITELY WILL CAUSE MISSCARRIAGE!!!**
Motherwort;	Acts as a uterine stimulant Avoid!
MUGWORT;	**VERY DANGEROUS** Is known to cause FETAL ABNORMALITIES!! Can also harm babies through BREAST FEEDING!!

Oshá.;	Has **sterols & saponins**. These are in doses that far exceed the safety factor for pregnancy
Pennyroyal;	**VERY DANGEROUS: DEFINITELY WILL CAUSE MISSCARRIAGE!!!**
Peony;	**VERY DANGEROUS: DEFINITELY WILL CAUSE MISSCARRIAGE!!!**
Rue oil;	**VERY DANGEROUS: DEFINITELY WILL CAUSE MISSCARRIAGE!!!**
Shepherd's Purse;	**DO NOT** drink or ingest during early pregnancy, acts as a uterine stimulant.
Thyme oil;	**DO NOT** use during early pregnancy, acts as a uterine stimulant
Unicorn Root;	*Use Caution* MAY POSSIBLY CAUSE MISCARRIAGE!!
Unicorn Root, False;	*Use Caution* MAY POSSIBLY CAUSE MISCARRIAGE!!
Vervain;	**DO NOT** drink or ingest during early pregnancy, acts as a uterine stimulant.
Wood Betony;	**DO NOT** drink or ingest during early pregnancy, acts as a uterine stimulant.
WORMWOOD;	**VERY DANGEROUS** Is known to cause FETAL ABNORMALITIES!! Can also harm babies through BREAST FEEDING!!
Yarrow;	**DO NOT** drink or ingest during early pregnancy, acts as a uterine stimulant.

Class #6
How to use a "Talking Board" in Spirit Contact

By: Lady Wolfen Mists © Oct.08, 1994

There are many types of 'Talking Boards 'out there for your use and they are **very** tempting to use. After all what harm can there be in talking to the spirits? Well, you can cause yourself a lot of grief and trouble if you use the boards with this type of attitude. This is a tool used in divination, and like all tools one needs to know how to operate it properly to get the desired effects. Talking boards are "tricky" to say the least, and can often draw energies that one would rather not be involved with. My advice to you is, if you have not been specifically trained by an instructor on the use, care and storage of a board then, **don't buy one.**

I recommend that you **NOT** use this tool until you are ready, but I know that many of you will try it out any way. The following information is meant to aid you in your explorations. I have attempted to educate you in such a way as to attract only positive energies to you and the board. However this is **Not Fool Proof.** It is only a precaution. I would like to restate the warning that this tool is often taken to lightly by the general public and should not be used unless one has been trained thoroughly on the techniques of its use. Remember when using any form of divination tool it is important to create a sacred space around you. One where you call the 4 directions to join in and help as well as protect you. Then call in your Higher Deity. In this case asking the Goddess and God to come and help you, protect you and guide you, to aid in your work. Be sure when creating your sacred sphere that you **"see"** it surrounding you and your tools, Creating a barrier that only positive energies can flow through. Once this is done you can move on with working with the tool.

What to do when first opening your Talking Board

First upon opening the board wipe the back of the board with purification/Holy water. Although making Metaphysical correct Holy water takes a number of steps and quite a few ingredients here's a quick recipe that you can easily whip up and use with success.

Mixture is approx. 1 quart (water distilled is best) to 1/2 teaspoon (salt), stir well.

Next take a cotton ball and put some water on it. As you lightly wipe the board and pointer down, visualize all the negative energies leaving and only positive energy being's able to communicate with you.

Then store box, pointer and board, in white clothe. A white pillowcase works well, for this. Storing the board like this when not in use, "sets" the positive energies and reinforces the board as a receiver for only positive energy exchanges. Inside the pillowcase you can sprinkle some salt (sea salt is best but any kind will do,) if you feel the need, especially after a long session of use.

What to do if you happen to get a Negative Spirit speaking to you?

If you get an entity that does not seem positive all is not lost and the board is not cursed. You just must take defensive action, like when you find termites in your house. You don't chuck out the house you exterminate the bugs.

So getting rid of your negative spirit is pretty simple if the infestation is new and of normal negative amounts. First do the above wipe down with the water/salt and then burn sage or sandalwood incense and "smudge" the board. That is to pass the board through the smoke a few times, telling the Entity, to leave and never return to you or your board. That it is unwelcome and must depart now. Also tell it to never try to harm you or yours again as you will not allow this to happen.

The entity **Will leave** and **Will Not** return, **as it must**, because **YOU** are in control of the situation. It is only when you give way to fear that you allow the entity to have power over you.

You need to know that **Nothing** can **Hurt** you that **You** do not **Let** or **Accept. Tell It To Go Now!** It will, **it has NO Choice!**

So remember, **Every time** you use the board, wipe it and the pointer down. Visualize only positive entities speaking with you, and store it in white. However if you feel uneasy with this and that you aren't up to the level to do this you can either send it to me and we will cleanse it for a small fee or you can bury it and leave it there forever. The Mother will reclaim the energies and send them back to the universe.

However **NEVER NEVER BURN IT**! Burning just sets the energies free into your Earth plane and they go out looking for some place else to infest. Many Metaphysical practitioner make this mistake, they think burning will destroy the entity, not so it just empowers it more and set it loose if you will. It is better, if you wish to rid yourself of the board completely without successful cleansing. To re attune it to the Earth (dig a hole and cover it) this allows the

Mother to do as She sees fit with the mis-aligned (negative) energies and you are safe from being followed by negative energies also.

Another point I'd like to make is **DO NOT EVER** use the board when drinking or doing mind altering drugs, as this is a magnet for negativity and drags these negative energies to you. If you wish to have meaningful contact with positive spirits, then YOUR life needs to reflect that. Otherwise you may as well get a neon sign and put it at the entrance of your open portal, and let every wondering negative energy suck energy out of you. As you can see by reading this, I hope, that working with "Talking Boards" includes alot of responsibility. It's not a tool to be taken lightly of, Please keep this in mind when working with yours

May You Always Walk In The Light,
Lady Wolfen Mists

Class #6
Test yourself

© Lady Wolfen Mists 2000© Lady Wolfen Mists 2000

Do Soul Sending Rite write in your Grimoire about it

1. What is a soul-sending rite used for?

2. Name and explain the types of spirit guides.

3. What is the Summerland?

4. List 4 of the traditional Sabbat herbs and what Sabbat they are used for.

5. List 4 of the Dangerous herbs for pregnant women & some of the possible side effects those herbs may cause

True or False (with respect to lesson given)

6.____ Spirit Boards should be used at wild parties, around alcohol.

7.____ Spirit Boards are only toys and are safe for anyone to play with

8.____ Spirit Boards should be stored in the color white.

9.____ If its herbal it's OK for anyone to take, no worries about side effects.

10. Write a short paragraph on the Soul Sending rite and tell me how it went.

Wolfen Wicca ®
Class #7

© Lady Wolfen Mists Jan.1990

revised 2000

Class #7

Theory;

Spell to aid in Removing Troubles

13 goals of a Witch

Creation Myths

Meditation: ***To see your Spirit Guide***

(Optional- Use Kitaro Light of the Spirit here)

Pendulums

Practical;

Test

Give the Spirit Guide Meditation a try write about it in your Grimoire

Class #7
Earth Work; Spell to Remove Troubles

© Lady Wolfen Mists Jan.1998

Materials required:

Ribbons for different reasons

Tree or shrub outside

Incense (*optional)

This spell is to aid in removing troubles from your life. It can be done at any moon phase and during the daytime

First determine what is bothering you and what you would like to see leave your life. For example, money problems or physical illness can be problems you chose to work with. Then pick a color that best represents that problem to you, (i.e. dark green could be money problems. Black could be physical illness.) Once this is done cut 1-2 foot Ribbons of the colors chosen to represent the problems. You can have as many problems represented as you like, just make sure there's a ribbon for each, set these aside.

Visualize these ribbons taking on all the characteristics of the problems that seem to be plaguing your life. These problems can be material, emotional, spiritual, anything or anyone. Also the colors you choose can be representative of one or more problems, there just MUST be 1 ribbon for each problem/concern.

Now go outside and find a tree or shrub you can 'tie" your problems to. If you can't find one around your living space try a park or out in the country. If this is still not possible you can buy a potted plant or shrub and place it by a door or window where the wind can easily reach it. Anyway pick your tree/shrub spot and go and get your problem ribbons from inside where you left them.

   Return with the ribbons to your tree/shrub. If you want to use incense in this spell here would be the time. Light the stick incense at this point as a tribute to air, letting it waft about. However incense isn't really necessary to get the spell to work. Begin to tie the ribbons to the top of the branches of the tree or shrub, you can tie as many ribbons to the same branch as you like or as the tree can bear. I however like to space the ribbons a bit giving each plenty of room to blow in the wind. The more room they have to blow the more complete the spell can be. Keep visualizing all the qualities and characteristics of your problems being "set" into the ribbon, as you tie them on. When this is complete spread your arms wide and say;

Sister Air hear my plea

Blow these troubles away from me

By the ribbon I have bound

A free new life will be found!

So by the powers inside me,

Thank you Air

So Mote It Be!

   Now your spell is cast and you are finished, just leave. Allow the ribbons to stay as long as they need, the wind will blow them away or someone else will remove them. If your tree is inside it is best to allow the sunlight to fade the ribbons to a very pale shade and then remove them much later. I know that sometimes it's impossible to do things outside but this is one of those times that it really does work better outdoors.

   This spell may take a while to work 2-4 months is not unusual, but don't lose faith if visualized properly it will work! Also you can always re-energize your ribbons if you like at any time, just visualize again over them. If you want you can re-do the entire spell adding more energy to it.

            Bright Blessings & Spell success to you all

                Lady Wolfen Mists

Class #7

Lady Wolfen Mists interpretation of 13 Goals of a Witch

© Lady Wolfen Mists Jan.1998

This is my interpretation of the Traditional 13 Goals of a Witch, read it and see how well you can or have incorporated it into your life. These 13 goals are important to the foundation of any beginner, and an excellent reminder for the advanced student, as well.

The 13 Goals of a Witch

© **Lady Wolfen Mists 1998**

In every major occurrence in our lives we have goals, to which we strive, so that we may achieve that final special outcome. That is what the 13 goals of a witch encompasses, ways that we may use to help us reach the highest spiritual aspiration's we can, while still on the mundane, physical world. The following is my interpretation of the traditional 13 goals of a Witch, read it and see how well you can or have incorporated it into your life.

1. Know yourself; don't be afraid to be who you are

2. Know your Craft (Wicca), be sure of what you know and don't be afraid to say there are things you don't know

3. Learn--Don't be afraid to try new things, to reach beyond your limits and to learn daily.

4. Apply knowledge with wisdom, Wisdom with compassion, compassion with discipline and discipline with love.

5. Achieve balance- Balance =Harmony and it is the way of the Universe.

6. Keep your words pure and clean, keep your promises for it is your bond.

7. Keep your thoughts as pure as possible, look with love as often as you can.

8. Celebrate life- it is a wonderful gift from the Lady and Lord. Take advantage of it and learn all you can while you are here.

9. Breath with the cycles of the Earth, it will set you to the rhythm of the universe and teach you the way of balance and harmony.

10. Breathe and eat correctly it will aid in you growth on all levels.

11. Exercise the body, do not allow it to stagnate and become withered.

12. Meditate often, it allows us to experience other places and hone our skills

13. Honor the Goddess and God daily. Honor yourself and others, and whatever path they choose to worship on, for in honoring all life then you honor the Lady & Lord

Who Is Out There???
Mom Can You See Me?

Class #7
Goddess Creation Stories

© Lady Wolfen Mists Jan. 1998

I have compiled a few different creation stories for you here. I want to make it clear I did not write them or take credit for them in any way. Quite simply they are fun to read and give the reader much to think about. I hope you enjoy them.

Armaiti, Lady of Green

This story comes from the Zoroastrian religion of ancient Persia

Dawn rises. Frost glitters, melts to beads of dew. Dew warms and mist forms, cool and clinging. Through the mist of spring moves Armaiti, steps quiet and bright. Her smile is warmer than the sun, golden and life loving. The land warms as the sun rises higher. Shadows creep away, sinking into hollows. Mountain slopes brighten, warm brown and reddish.

From the horizon of the rising sun steps Armaiti. She is the Daughter of Truth and Light, Ahura Mazda. She is Devotion, Lady of Rebirth and Spring. From the dead places She calls forth life, coaxing it from the cold winter soil with gentle words and warm hands.

She is Devotion. Slumbering trees waken and bud, and Her smile brightens. Fragile shoots push through reluctant soil, and Her steps grow light. Stems bud and flower blooms open, petals fragrant and colorful. Hills green as She treads their slopes. Her breath is perfume, deep red and yellow. The wind catches it and carries it away, mixes it with the perfume of the rose and the lotus, the lilac and the lily. Round the hills the perfume blows, to old trees and stumps. Bees waken and buzz from their hives, and Armaiti laughs.

She is Devotion. She calls the world to life. She calls the seedlings to rise from the ground, to spread their leaves in the loving light of the sun. She calls the world to praise Ahura Mazda, Father of Light and Truth. Birds sing in glory. Bees buzz, streaks of gold and black. Flowers bob heavy heads, and leaves unfurl, spreading in His light. Snow melts and streams run clear and rapid, glittering in His light. She is Armaiti. She calls the world to life.

Benzozia, Mother Dragon

This story is from the Basque people of northern Spain.

The world was a cold, flat place then. There were no mountains or valleys or sea. There was no warmth, only cold wind blowing across an endless plain. Beneath the earth lived Benzozia, Mother Dragon. She was a great serpent, with seven great jaws and fourteen great fangs. Beneath the earth, Benzozia slept. But Her sleep was restless. She turned in Her sleep and Her great scales rasped against the earth above. Her heavy coils, all shades of red and blue and purple, arched against the earth above, and the earth groaned.

Again and again, Benzozia turned in Her sleep. Her heavy coils pushed against the earth above, arched and shoved. The earth groaned and moved. The earth split wide and rose high. Into the cold air the earth rose in peaks, and the Pyrenees were created, the world's first mountains.

In Her sleep, Benzozia rolled and from Her seven great jaws fire poured forth. It rose up, poured through the cracks in the earth and erupted from mountains and valleys. It rolled across the surface of the earth, luminous gas and burning liquid. It burned the soil and the air. It burned hot and clouds rose, mixtures of dust and moisture. Water fell from the clouds created of Benzozia's fire. The fire and water fought and hissed and more clouds were born, and the fire began to retreat, back down into the earth. Water filled the low

places and mixed with earth burned dark black by fire. Trees and bushes pushed tiny shoots through the dark soil and lifted their heads into the air. Taller and taller they grew, no longer driven to hide beneath the ground by the cold above.

Into the earth the fire retreated. But from its sparks, its warm embers and hot gas and hot liquid, came the first people. There were the Basque, born of Benzozia's fire.

She lives still, the Great Mother Dragon, beneath the earth. Her sleep is still restless and the earth groans when She pushes with Her heavy coils. From time to time, She opens Her great jaws in Her sleep and fire erupts forth. It sweeps up through cracks and crevices in the earth; but now it erupts only from the heights of mountains, far from the low places filled with water.

Citlalicue, Lady Star Skirt

This story comes from the ancient Aztec culture. Oh and just so you know Citlalicue means "Star Skirt," she is considered the embodiment of the Milky Way.

Some say the Milky Way is a river, a river of light that the Gods sail in their nightly voyage. Others say it is a road, the Highway of the Gods. Still other peoples say it is a sash or a cloak or the milk of a Goddess. But the Aztecs know that the flowing stream is Citlalicue, Mother of the Gods.

It is said that Citlalicue birthed a knife of flint. In a gush of red blood, the knife of firestone came forth, gray-black. By this flint knife, Citlalicue became the Mother of all the Gods and Goddesses. She became the Mother of Them All, one thousand six hundred in all.

To the depths of the earth descended Citlalicue, flint knife in Her hand, into the caverns of the earth. There, She smeared the knife of firestone with the blood of Her womb. Into a bowl of cool blue light Citlalicue dipped the knife, into a bowl of light like the ocean. From the bowl stepped forth beings noble and upright. The first

humans arose from the bowl of blue light, the parents of the noble Aztecs. From the bowl arose two Deities. These two Deities, noble children of Citlalicue, set themselves aflame. The elder burned with a fire golden-red and hot. He rose into the sky and became the Sun; He shines for us yet today. The younger burned with a cooler fire, white-blue and gray. He rose into the sky and became the Moon; He shines for us yet today.

And so the order of the universe was set in motion. Sun shines at day, warming crops and land. Moon shines at night, guiding the traveler. And through the dark sky arches the stream of stars, which is fair Citlalicue, Mother of the Gods.

Gaea, Mother Earth

This story tells of the ancient Greek Deity Gaea (or Gaia or Ge).

Before time, there is only Chaos. Formless, heavy mixes with light, darkness with bright, earth and air and fire and water, undifferentiated.

Then Gaea creates Herself. She pulls Her being from primal Chaos by the force of Her will. She wills Herself into existence. Gaea separates the heavy and the light, the dark and the bright, the elements of earth and air and fire and water. The lighter She sets above, the heavier below. From fire She forms the sun and stars. From the heavier She forms the planets. From the heavier She creates a form for Herself and calls it Earth. Air settles around Her in a warm, blue blanket. Water fills Her low places, salty and fresh. Clouds form, and rain falls. Earth grows moist and from Her depths Gaea brings forth trees and shrubs, vines and herbs. Animals of all variety are born, called forth by Gaea: deer and bear, bird and mouse, horse and pig. She populates Her seas and lakes and rivers with fish of all kinds, and crabs and urchins and dolphins and jellyfish. Gaea looks upon Her creation, and is glad.

For uncounted time, Gaea is joyful in Her creation. She watches mountain slopes green in spring. She watches mountain peaks glisten with winter's snow. She listens to the mating song of birds and the undersea song of the whale. She feels the unsteady tread of sleepy bear steps as winter melts into spring. She smells the tangy scent of berries carried by autumn winds.

Gaea is joyous with Her creation. She desires to share it with another like Herself. And so She calls forth another, molding Him of fire and of air. Uranus She calls Him, son and lover. And Gaea discovers new joys with Her creation.

Honored High Mistress

This is from Siberia. You may notice it has many of the same symbolism found in the Christian Bible (Book of Genesis) yet that is where the parallel ends, the interpretation here is much different.

At the center of the world, at the navel of the universe, there grows a great Eight-Branched Tree. Its trunk is gnarled and knotted and golden-brown. Its roots grow deep into the earth of the cosmos. Its branches, thick and heavy, grow high into the heavens. Within the branches of the great Eight-Branched Tree lives White Youth. He is the First Man. He eats of the leaves of the Tree, and the fruit, which hangs from its boughs.

But White Youth grows restless. He knows there is more--he knows there is something he must do. White Youth sits in the branches of the Tree and considers. He considers for a long time. Then he stands and climbs the branches of the Tree; he climbs higher and higher to the very topmost branch, and looks out upon the cosmos. White Youth sees broad plains of grass through which rivers curve. He sees far distant mountains and dense green forests.

He sees animals, too, furred and scaly and feathered. From the topmost branch of the Tree, White Youth looks upon the cosmos--and feels the first stirrings of curiosity.

I must see those mountains, he says. I must climb those trees, which are so much smaller. I must feel the grass beneath my feet and swim in the great rivers. I must meet these animals and feel their fur and feathers and scales with my hands.

And White Youth climbs back, back down the great Eight-Branched Tree at the navel of the universe. Down and down he climbs. He slides down the trunk and touches his feet to the earth, the First Man to feel earth beneath his feet.

The wind blows then. The leaves of the great Tree rustles and shakes. The Tree quakes and the whole cosmos shakes. The earth at the base of the Tree swells and cracks and a woman emerges. Her hair is long and black and fell the ground. Her skin is golden-warm. Her eyes are solemn.

Drink, she says, and offers Her breasts to White Youth. He drinks of Her milk until he is full. Then the woman steps back, and disappears, once more into the earth at the roots of the great Tree. And White Youth set off across the plains, First Man.

Shekinah, Wind Upon the Waters

This story of creation is difficult to find, though it is right at the beginning of the Book of Genesis. Centuries of accidental and deliberate mistranslation and ignorance of ancient Hebrew culture have obscured the feminine role in Judeo-Christian creation. At the height of the culture of Moorish Spain, Kabbalists (a sect of Judaism) returned to Shekinah Her important role in the creation of the universe, of children and of art.

POURING OUT THE STARS

I am Shekinah. I am the First Thought of YHWH. I am the Wisdom of YHWH. I am the Breath of YHWH. I am the Infinite Love of YHWH.

I am the First Thought of YHWH. I am the source of consciousness. I am She Who was there in the beginning, the very Thought of Creation, which YHWH conceived.

I am the Wisdom of YHWH. I am that which inspires all creation. I am She Who was there in the beginning, the intelligence which guided the creation of biosphere's, which designed the Laws of Nature, which determined the balance of living and dying.

I am the Breath of YHWH. I am that which enervates creation. I am She Who was there in the beginning, the wind, which moved upon still waters, the energy, which fueled the creation of suns and stars, lakes and mountains, forests and jungles.

I am the Infinite Love of YHWH. I am that which makes meaning of existence. I am She Who was there in the beginning, the love which made YHWH complete and which completes His Creation.

I am Shekinah. I am First Thought, the image of a painting which appears in an artist's mind, the image of a child which appears in a father's thoughts. I am Wisdom, which guides and inspires the paintbrush of the artist, the dancing steps of the dancer, the quill of the writer. I am Breath, which animates the babe in the womb, the pen upon paper, the sculptor's chisel upon hard marble. I am Infinite Love, which unites YHWH with His creation and His children with one another.

I am Shekinah. I am the face of the Unknowable, which may be known. I walk among the people, teaching them laws, teaching them arts, reminding them of the Infinite Love which inspired their creation and which inspires creation still. `I am Shekinah.'

Sothis, Mistress Flood

This story finds it way from ancient Egypt, It reflects an aspect of the Goddess Isis. Sothis is the name for Sirius, the Dog Star.

The Heaven, which is Nut's spangled body, covers the earth. She arches over it, on fingertips and tiptoes. Her body is ink black. White and red and green stars wink and twinkle on Her black body. She is Mistress Night, Wife of the Earth, Mother of the Sun.

Many are the stars, which wink and twinkle on Her body, of many colors and brightness. Many are the Divine figures, which the stars form: Osiris, Lord of the Dead, and Tauret, Mistress of Childbirth. It is to the stars that astrologer's look, to chart the destiny of newborn sons and daughters. It is to the stars that the sailor looks, to the fixed northern light, which guides him home.

But it is one star especially which draws the eye of potter and prostitute and Priestess and Pharaoh. That is the star, which rises in the east, shining bright, heralding the Inundation of the Nile, the beginning of the New Year.

Through the long nights, the priests keep anxious vigil. Night after night they watch for the star Sothis. Many are Her titles: the Arrow Star, Queen of the Thirty-Six Constellations, Star of the Sea, the Star of Isis. Many are Her names: Sopdet, Sept, Septet, Sirius. She is the Star of the Inundation. Mistress of the Flood.

Far distant from Egypt, rain falls upon the highlands of Ethiopia. Down the mountains the water runs, into the Blue Nile and the White Nile. The two great rivers converge and flow together, north

into the Great Green. The waters of the great Nile swell, filled with the rain of the highlands. Over its banks the Nile sweeps, across fields and boundaries. Beneath the silt-brown waters the fields lay for many weeks. Slowly, the waters recede, and the earth is rich and black again.

Back to their fields the farmers return, back to fields rejuvenated. To the Nile, the farmers offer their thanks. To Sothis, they offer their thanks, farmer and herdsman, potter and Pharaoh. To Sothis they offer praise, Lady of the Inundation, Who heralds the Rejuvenation of the Land.

Aataentsic, Sky Woman

A story of creation as told by the Iroquois.

Then, there was only infinite blue: sea merged into sky, one continuous dome of blue, above and below. There were clouds, too, wispy white and dark gray, which rained water into the limitless sea. Birds flew in and among the clouds, hovering in the wind, flapping madly and squawking as it gusted and threatened to toss them into the rolling waves. When they were not soaring in the blue of the sky, they were floating in the blue of the sea, squawking and peddling their flippered feet and diving beak-first to catch fish. The fish were many and varied, solid gray and stripped white and red and brilliant yellow with purple plumage. Upon the waves there lived then four other animals. Great Turtle was ancient and huge, his dark green and brown and black shell glistening wet; the other animals and the birds would rest upon it now and then when they were tired of floating or swimming or flying or wanted to rest their fish-filled bellies. Otter was there, too, and Muskrat, and old, ugly Grandmother Toad. Life was gentle and without adventure.... Until the woman fell from the sky.

    They did not realize at first that she was falling. Otter saw the reflection first, as he lay on his belly upon Great Turtle's back. He frowned when he saw the figure in the water, distant and tiny. He had never seen anything like it. He called over Muskrat and asked him, curiously, What did he think it was? Muskrat scratched his whiskered nose. Some sort of fish, he opined. Rising from the Bottom. Otter quivered with curiosity. The Bottom? He had never heard of this thing, the Bottom. Oh, yes, Muskrat assured him, quite pleased that he knew something Otter did not. It is quite far down, very far down. Otter peered into the water, at the thing rising from the Bottom. Have you ever seen it? Muskrat scowled, whiskers twitching. He reluctantly admitted that he had not. But I have heard some of the fish speak of it, he explained. I talk to them sometimes before I eat them. It's getting closer, said Otter. It will be at the top soon.

    Grandmother Toad swished around in the water before them. The water rippled, quivering the image of the creature rising from the Bottom. What is getting closer, she asked? Her voice was very deep. It reminded Otter of the deep silence of the sea, very far down where the blue turned to black. That thing coming out of the water, said Muskrat. Grandmother Toad dove suddenly. Otter and Muskrat watched her; they could see her green body, odd-shaped green legs kicking. She surfaced again, large eyes blinking. There is nothing down there.

    Muskrat's whiskers quivered with agitation. He insisted that of course there is, and dove into the water himself. He swam around frantically, tail swishing, going in circles deeper and deeper. Then, he surfaced, head gleaming dully. There's nothing there, he reported, sulking, as he was wont to do when a particularly delicious fish managed to get away.

    Otter frowned and thought very hard. He remembered the reflections of birds he had seen, swooping and diving. Well, if it's not coming up, he reasoned, perhaps its coming down! He rolled onto his back, turning his eyes to the great dome of blue that covered the whole universe, only clouds and birds in between. And there it was, an odd-shaped creature. It had no wings. It was falling quickly. It's falling, it's falling! exclaimed Muskrat. Birds began to squawk and

cry, more loudly then usual. ....*Falling, falling, falling*....they cried.....*No wings, no wings*.... What will happen to it when it reaches the water? wondered Otter aloud. It will die, said Grandmother Toad. The water is hard when one falls that fast. ....*Falling, falling, falling*.... It needs something else to fall on, said Otter.

They could hear the terrible sound now. It was a cry, not of a bird angry with the wind or at another fellow for plucking his tail feathers. It was a cry of fear and of terror, the first heard in the world.

Otter rose up on his hind legs, tail flapping agitatedly. Great Turtle's shell is too hard. It would hurt itself when it landed. The Bottom, then, said Muskrat.

The fish tell me its soft, some of them, when they go down that deep, they hit it with their tails sometimes and great clouds of the stuff spread through the water. Perhaps we could put some of it on Great Turtle's back, like putting a cloud there! Yes, yes! That's it! exclaimed Otter. We need some Bottom! Muskrat dove into the blue water. He swam deep, tail swishing rapidly, legs kicking. Deep he dove and deeper still, down to where the blue changed to purple. Down he dove, till his lungs hurt and his legs began to cramp. He could go no further. He turned, kicked as his legs began to hurt even more. The water changed back from purple to blue. His lungs hurt and his head hurt, and finally he was at the surface again, sucking in air. He had not reached the Bottom.

Otter dove next, from the shell of Great Turtle. Down deep he dove, through the blue sea, through the purple sea, to where the water began to blacken and the swishing of fish tails was seldom heard. But he could go no further: his legs hurt and his lungs hurt and even his great tail. He turned and returned to the surface, sucking in air. He had not reached the Bottom.

Lastly, Grandmother Toad dove through the waters. She dove through the blue waters and the purple waters and into the black waters, where the noise of fish tails was little heard. She dove deeper, into the black silence of the sea. It was cold. Her legs began to hurt, front legs and back. The water was heavy all around her. She did not

see the Bottom, for there was no light. She swam right into it, mouth and nostrils filling with its grainy coldness. She scooped it up into her mouth, almost choking. She filled her mouth with grains of the Bottom.

Up she began to swim, kicking her tired legs, paddling and pushing. The Bottom was heavy in her mouth, and cold. The water stayed black for a very long time. Grandmother Toad feared she would never see the infinite blue again. Then, slowly, the water began to lighten, from black to dark purple to lighter purple, to dark blue and finally to the lighter blue of the surface. Her head topped the waves and air touched her warty skin. She spat the Bottom out of her mouth, vomited it onto Great Turtle's back. She choked and coughed. Her tired legs stopped kicking, her tired legs stopped paddling, and she fell, back through the blue and purple and black waters, fell and fell and never returned.

The Bottom sat on Great Turtle's back. It was a lump of wet brown and black, very unattractive and lumpy. Otter and Muskrat stared at it, standing on their hind legs. The Bottom just sat there, drying in the wind. They could still hear the sound, the scream which grew louder and louder. The birds were screaming too, flapping about in agitation. Something terrible was going to happen. We need more Bottom, announced Muskrat.

Then something wonderful happened. The Bottom moved. It was not a very great move, not at first, just a sort of quiver. Then it plopped over, fell with a squish. And it began to grow. It rolled out over Great Turtle's back, spreading across the great hard shell. It grew and grew and grew, grew thicker and darker and wider, thicker in some places, thinner in others. It sent Otter and Muskrat scrambling over the side of Great Turtle's shell and into the blue water. They watched as it continued to grow. Look, look, look! Muskrat pointed excitedly.

Up in the sky, they could see the falling creature. It was much closer. It had great tangles of black fur growing out of its head and its belly was round, and it had four legs. It was much closer and the terrible sound was louder.

The birds screamed and called to one another. They flapped their wings and dove through the wind and among the clouds. They caught the creature's legs with their flipper feet, caught its black fur in their beaks, slipped beneath its falling body and supported it with theirs. The creature slowed in its fall, slowed, but was still falling. And the terrible sound was getting louder.... The Bottom continued to grow. It was thick and black in some places, dried and brown in others, even reddish. And then it stopped growing.

The crash of the thing onto the Bottom on Great Turtle's back was terrible. The Bottom rippled and squished. Great Turtle moaned. Great Turtle sank into the infinite blue and water spilled over the Bottom which covered his back. The creature choked and coughed as the water washed over it. Then Great Turtle rose again and the water fell away. Great waves washed through the infinite blue of the sea, swift-moving circles, pushing at Muskrat and Otter and the many fish which swam about. Then the water stilled, and it was very quiet. Otter and Muskrat began to creep forward. There was a great clatter and rain fell, across the back of Great Turtle. They were hard little balls of many colors and sizes. Brown clumps like Bottom fell, too, and green tangles of plant like that which floated in the infinite sea. They splashed and plopped, the hard balls and clumps and tangles, and buried themselves in the Bottom.

Muskrat and Otter raised their heads from beneath the waves. They crept out of the blue water. The Bottom squished beneath their paws and between their toes. They crept over to the creature. The creature was sleeping. Then it began to cry.

I am Aataentsic, the creature said. I am of the Ongwe, the People of the Sky. We live high above, beyond the blue dome. I am the mate of Earth-Holding Chief. I went to him at the counsel of my father's spirit. I passed many tests to prove my worthiness. But, after we mated, he sent me away. I returned to my people. When my body began to swell, they became angry. They threw me from the Land of the Ongwe. I fell. I fell. I fell. I screamed, at my father for sending me to Earth-Holding Chief, at Earth-Holding Chief for his cruelty, at the people for their shame. I screamed in anger, I screamed in fear. Then the birds grabbed me with their flipper feet and their beaks. Then I awakened here.

Her body tightened then and pain spiked her belly. Her blood mixed with the dark brown and black grains of the Bottom and Her daughter slid forth. She placed Her daughter on Her belly and wiped Her clean. Her daughter cried and the wind blew, and so Aataentsic named her daughter Gusts of Wind. Upon the back of Great Turtle They lived, Mother and Daughter. Gusts of Wind grew and Her belly rounded, though She had no mate. Twins came forth, while pain spiked Her belly and legs, golden and silver. They rose into the sky, glowing with light, the sun and the moon, and so measurable Time came to the world, day and night. The dome was no longer blue, but black also. Spark's of light shone in the blackness, holes, which the Ongwe had poked through the dome with their planting sticks as they planted their corn and squash.

The seeds, which had fallen with Aataentsic, clawed free of celestial soil, took root in the mud of the Bottom. They rose in the warm light of the sun, oaks and elms and willow, berry bushes and herbs. They spread across the Bottom, which covered the round shell of Great Turtle, covering the thick places and the thin, covering mountains and valleys, growing round the low places which had filled with water when Great Turtle moaned.

Upon the back of Great Turtle they lived, Mother and Daughter, as we still live. Their bellies rounded and children came forth, sons and daughters, though they had no mates. The planting of corn and squash Aataentsic taught them, the gathering of bark and herbs. Respect for women's ways and women's wisdom, Aataentsic taught them. Sons mated with daughters and bronze-skinned children were born. In the forests they lived, and beside the lakes and rivers, upon the back of Great Turtle who lives in the sea.

__Lower Kingdom Creation Myth__ Egyptian myth

Only the ocean existed at first. Then Ra (the sun) came out of an egg that appeared on the surface of the water. Ra brought forth four children, the gods Shu and Geb and the Goddesses Tefnut and Nut. Shu and Tefnut became the

atmosphere. They stood on Geb, who became the earth, and raised up Nut, who became the sky. Ra ruled over all. Geb and Nut later had two sons, Set and Osiris, and two daughters, Isis and Nephthys. Osiris succeeded Ra as king of the earth, helped by Isis, his sister-wife. Set, however, hated his brother and killed him. Isis then embalmed her husband's body with the help of the god Anubis, who thus became the god of embalming. The powerful charms of Isis resurrected Osiris, who became king of the netherworld, the land of the dead. Horus, who was the son of Osiris and Isis, later defeated Set in a great battle and became king of the earth.

(Upper Kingdom creation story)

At first there was only *Nun*, the primal ocean of chaos that contained the beginnings of everything to come. From these waters came Ra who, by himself, gave birth to Shu and Tefnut. Shu, the god of air, and Tefnut, the Goddess of moisture gave birth to Geb and Nut, the earth god and the sky Goddess. And so the physical universe was created. Men were created from Ra's tears. They proved to be ungrateful so Ra, and a council of gods, decided they should be destroyed. Re created Sekhmet to do the job. She was very efficient and slaughtered all but a few humans, when Ra relented and tricked her into stopping. Thus was the present world created. Against Ra's orders, Geb and Nut married. Ra was incensed and ordered Shu to separate them, which he did. But Nut was already pregnant, although unable to give birth as Ra had decreed she could not give birth in any month of any year. Thoth, the god of learning, decided to help her and gambling with the moon for extra light, was able to add five extra days to the 360-day calendar. On those five days Nut gave birth to Osiris, Horus the Elder, Set, Isis, and Nephthys successively. Osiris became the symbol of good, while Set became the symbol of evil. And thus the two poles of morality were fixed once and for all.

Creation Theories---Author Unknown

Once long ago, before people roamed Mother Earth, there was only the utter stillness of darkness. Then came a sound, and with the sound a light, but the light grew stronger, darkness retreated in fear. Something miraculous happened next, the light split into two and became two distinct entities, separate, yet one. One entity took the form of a man crowned with the antlers of a mighty stag. The other, a woman who shown with the radiance of a full Moon on a cloudless night. These are they who Witches call the Lord and Lady, God and Goddess, They are known by many names yet, they are one in the same.

Then the Goddess went to darkness and declared it name, and in doing so absorbed it into her, creating the Universal womb, thus allowing the people of the World a chance of re-birth.

On seeing the Lady do this deed, Love was woken in the heart of the Lord and they joined together in love. Both of them climaxing together in a great shower of ecstasy, creating the physical Universe and all of it. The stars are the seed of the Lord, fertilizing the womb of the mother, so as these word are written, new worlds of life and new worlds and life are ever being brought forth in a continuous cycle of life, death, and re-birth. In order for something to be born, something must die. This is a universal law that cannot be changed. There is no need to fear death; it is merely a doorway to the universal womb to await rebirth, a chance for rest following lives often-hard journey through the material world.

Next the Lord and Lady set the order of the Seasons and declared eight festivals be observed to mark their turning, for the year is like a wheel rolling down the road, constantly flowing one after another. First comes Samhain the feast of the dead, next is Yule to celebrate the birth of the young Lord, followed by Imbolc the first signs of spring, next is Ostara when day and night are equal, Beltane is next to celebrate life, love and the warm days of Summer, Litha follows to celebrate the high days of Summer and the Summer King's ascendancy, Lammas first of the harvest festivals, and finally comes

Mabon the second of the harvest fairs. The Lord then decreed the time of the full Moon to honor the Lady, Life, Love and Magick.

As the God and Goddess created the year, so they also created night and day. They declared that the Sun should rule the day, physical labor and all souls. The Moon should rule the night, magick, and emotions. There is nothing to fear in the night, children, for it is a necessary opposite to the day, revel in her beauty and mystery.

Looking at their creation they saw how beautiful it was. For the Earth is indeed Beautiful, a jewel in the blackness of the universal womb. They created all manor of animals to place on the Earth Mother including Man and Woman. Next they decreed they should be stewards of their new creation. In order for man and woman to carry out the task in harmony each with the other, they taught them Magick.

Class #7
Seeing your Spirit Guide

© Lady Wolfen Mists Jan.1998

<u>Materials required</u>:

- A safe place to sit where you will be undisturbed. Take the phone off the hook
- Book of Shadows & pen to record what happens.
- Stick incense placed in a safe place where it wont catch anything on fire (*optional)
- Kitaro Music---Light of the Spirit (*optional}
- Something to play the music on (*optional)
- Tissues as this can get emotional (happy at finally meeting)
- Something to drink (in case you need to cough also great when you get back)
- Something to eat (any time you do astral/psychic work you may find you get the munchies. Have something ready really helps)

Once you are all set and prepared, this is what you do. Read this entire sheet first and follow the steps as closely as possible, Take your time, try to imagine as much detail as possible.

1. Sit in a comfortable position, one that you can sustain for about 30 minutes. Lying down is all right but you may fall a sleep in this position.

2. Close your eyes and take in a deep cleansing breath, begin the 4-count breathing (See class #1 for details on this) you were taught, at your own speed. Pull down the white light (See Arms of the Lady for details class #2)

3. Once in the arms of the Lady ask that you see ask your guides and teachers. Ask to be sat in your safe place, at a place where they can come to you. State your intention clearly and ask the Goddess to help you with your journey.

4. See your self at your safe place, You might find yourself sat down on a rock or by a pond or in a great tree, anywhere. Just sit there and wait. Your main Spirit Guide will come.

5. As you sit there you may see a swirl of colored energy coming your way. It may appear white or purple, green or electric blue. It comes to you.

6. It hovers over you for a few seconds. You may think you hear laughter or even a voice. You will have a "knowing" inside you if this presence is male, female or both. It will then manifest itself in front of you. Its shape may be familiar to you or it may be unusual. Do not fear you are in your safe place and nothing harmful to you can be here. So relax and go with the flow

7. If you are lucky the spirit guide will manifest completely (this usually doesn't happen the first time so don't feel bad if it doesn't) You may get to see the face, shape clearly and they may speak with you. Speaking is another thing that doesn't happen right away, as you both need to focus energy to do this and right now you may not be able to do it very well as you are emotionally excited that its working and a bit frightened. As you work more and this becomes "old hat" to you, you will focus better and get better results

8. Your Guide may speak with you are give you some instructions in your mind. Listen well, and remember. They will also give you your first gift to be placed at your safe place. It can be anything, but they will give you something. Accept it and say thank you.

9. Spend as much or as little time as you need there, but remember now that you know the way you can visit them any time you like.

10. Before coming back to this plane be sure to thank the Goddess and you Spirit Guide. Place your gift in a place of honor in your safe place and say good bye.

11. Be sure to ground upon your return (see class # 2 for details) and Welcome back.

Upon return you may want to write in your Book of Shadows everything that happened. Any name you may have gotten concerning your spirit guide and any information you may have been given. Also write what it was that you were given and what it may do if you were told.

If you want to return to your safe place at any time, since you know the way its simple. Just call down the white light and ill yourself to your safe place. Call your spirit guide and they will come.

It's that simple and with practice and focus you will become quite efficient at doing this. Don't be discouraged if things don't go perfectly right away. You are learning and this takes focus and concentration. You are seeing so many things for the first time and experiencing so many new feelings, sights and sounds that your not as focused as you need to be. That's perfectly ok and you will learn to become more focused and concentrated as you experience more. DO NOT shame yourself or think you are a failure just because it didn't go exactly as planned. Enjoy these first excursions, it's like seeing through the eyes of a child. Delight in seeing things as you are and allow yourself freedom to grow as your own rate. Do not ruin this by placing expectations on yourself. ENJOY and make this as stress free as possible!

Class #7
The Pendulum as a Tool

By: Lady Wolfen Mists © 08-07-91 revised 03-30

The pendulum is an extremely old divination and dowsing tool. It is used to trigger the intuition of the user and connect to the "higher Self" This is done by bring forth information from the subconscious to the conscious level and allowing us to become aware of the information via the pendulum. Thus, in essence, the information from the pendulum comes from deep within ourselves. The pendulum acts as a center of focus that we may access these many levels of information found in the subconscious.

When you are working with a pendulum, as with any form of divination tool, it is important to create a sacred space around you. A space where you call the 4 directions to join in, and help as well as protect you. Then call in your Higher Deity. In this case asking the Goddess and God to come help, protect, and guide you. Be sure when creating your sacred sphere that you **"see"** it surrounding you and your tools, Creating a barrier that only positive energies can flow through. It also helps that you clean your tools before and after their use, keeping them clean of residual energies helps to insure a positive experience.

To use the pendulum you first need to lay down a lettered circle. Anoint the pendulum with Activation Oil (see Silver Hoofs and ask for this.) Then pick up the chain of the pendulum, with your dominant hand, and allow it to hang down between your fingers becoming familiar with the pendulum. Notice the color and the texture of the pendulum itself, become aware of how it hangs and what it feels like in your hands. Once you have done this visualize your energies and the energies of the pendulum coming together as one, working as one, yet coming from two separate entities.

Once this is done, take the chain between your thumb and forefinger. Extend your forearm out over the lettered circle. **DO NOT**

LEAN on your elbow, as this interferes with the true flow of energy. Now approx. 2 inches above the center of the circle allow the pendulum to hang. If the pendulum seems to swing too much and wont still, you may touch it down to the center of the circle.

However be sure to raise it again approx. 2 inches up over the circle once you have stilled it. Take your opposite (non-dominate) hand, and place it palm down on the table surface. You are now ready to "Tune" you pendulum.

Tuning A Pendulum

Tuning a pendulum consists of asking as serious of questions that you already know the answers to, and learning from your pendulum's swing, which way means yes and which way means no. Answers from different pendulums may mean different types/directions of swings. A swing can be clock wise or counterclockwise or back and forth or even sideways. So this is why you need to tune you pendulum, so you may be able to read its answers correctly. So your first questions should be one that you **know** the answer is **yes** to.

For example ask aloud: "Am I female?" Assuming you are female the answer would be yes and the pendulum would begin to swing in a direction that will be read as yes, from now on. You can repeat a yes answered questions several times so you are sure to get an accurate reading on which direction is yes. Once the direction of yes is established to your satisfaction mark it down on the outside of the letter circle.

Next you need to establish the direction of No. To do this you ask out loud a question that you **know** the answer is **no** to. For example; "Am I (untrue age) years old?" Again notice the direction and mark it, as you may ask a serious of questions to establish a direction, for certain. Once the direction is established this will be the no signal for this pendulum from now on.

As you work with your pendulum you will become more aware of "how it works", its personality and its energy flow.

Soon you will be able to use it to have it spell things out for you, tell you directions and even find things/people for you on maps. However you will **need much practice** with it often. You need to build a rapport between you and your pendulum to achieve successful results on a regular basis.

Now looking at the actual pendulum itself you will notice that there is room for a stone on each end of the chain. This extra stone can be placed there to add its properties or qualities to the reading, both stones are chosen for their harmonious interaction with one another. You may even use this stone in some cases instead of the pendulum cone end when asking something that is central it the stones properties/qualities.

To use the stone so that it may aid the crystal pendulum in the reading, hold the chain between thumb and forefinger. The last three fingers need to "cup" the stone inside of your palm.

One last area to note is that, as you grow in expertise with your pendulum, the pendulum will respond more and more to your questions. It may even reveal its true name to you, however this may take quite awhile. In the meantime you need to concentrate on building a trusting relationship between you and your pendulum. When it comes to cleansing you will need to set your pendulum in water every 30 days or so, this can be done on the full moon for two reasons. First reason is that it's a regular occurring date that you can remember when you last cleaned your pendulum on. Secondly the full moon energies cleanse and energize the energies of the crystal and the stone as it sets in the moonlight. The method is simple, just select a glass and add distilled or spring water into the glass, enough to cover the pendulum. Put the pendulum into the water and allow the glass to sit in the moonlight, (i.e. open window with moonlight flowing through) until the morning. Remove the pendulum from the glass, dry it off and put it away. Then empty the water outside on the ground and your good for about another 30 days or so. In so cases, as you get to know your pendulum, you'll know when it needs cleaned. This

may be more often then 30 days or longer then 30 days, in any case the method is pretty much the same. Just put it in distilled or spring water overnight and dry off in the morning. Well I'll leave you now and let you get acquainted with your

new pendulum, remember to **Practice Often!**

A Side Note: Also be sure to speak your intent about want to do only positive work and to associate with only positive spirits. When you are finished with your session "Thank" all the directions for coming and helping you and tell them to go now, Then most humbly thank your Higher Deity for their help and tell them you are finished and they may go if they like. Place your tools in where they will be cleaned, like a bowl of distilled water and end the session. Clean your tools regularly and when in doubt always store your items in WHITE. You can also apply a protection oil, or even burn special types of incense, to/around yourself and your tools to aid in creating a sacred space if you are in a situation where the actual creation of such a space would cause you to be uncomfortable

May You Always Walk In The Light,

Lady Wolfen Mist

Class #7
Test What you have learned

© Lady Wolfen Mists 2000

Use other paper if needed

1. Where does the information from the pendulum, in essence, come from?

2. What do you think is the two most important goals in the 13 goals of a witch & why?

3. What was your favorite "Creation story" and why?

4. Write your own creation story, you can also draw a series of pictures if you feel that would better explain your creation story. Use additional paper please and be sure to put your name on the story.

5. Write a short paragraph on your Spirit Guide Meditation for your Grimoire

Wolfen Wicca ®
Class #8

© Lady Wolfen Mists Jan.1990
revised 2000

Class #8

Theory;

Types of Magick;
  Sympathetic Magick
  Contagious Magick

Power

Invocation for Law of 3

Consecration

Rite of Consecration of Tools

Dream Pillow Recipe

Practical;

Test

Do Consecration ritual for item &
  ***write in your Grimoire how it went

Class #8

Magickal Approaches

© Lady Wolfen Mists Jan.1998

Now that you have an understanding of power, lets move on to magickal approaches. There are many ways to approach magick but for our use here we will discuss the 2 major styles. They are called Sympathetic Magick and Contagious Magick.

Sympathetic Magick

This style is based on the Law of Similarity. What this law says is that what happens to one thing is likely to happen to another.

Examples of this would be:

A voodoo doll (poppet magick) the reason being is that it resembles the person.

A candle made into an item of similarity, like a cat candle for your cat familiar or such

So anything that is similar to the person or thing that you want to do magick on. You would use this item in place of the person and what happened to it would act similarly to the person in question.

Contagious Magick

This style is based on the Law of Contact. What this law says is that what happens to something that has been in contact with a person will continue to have affects on that person's life.

Examples of this would be:

Clothing of the person work

Hair/nail clipping

Any item having had close personal contact. The closer the contact (like underwear) and the longer the contact (like a special pen used daily by them) the better it will work.

So here anything that the person touches or uses or wears regularly (the longer the better) can be used to cast magick on. Whatever happens to these items there will be a contagious effect on the person.

Now before you ask yes you can combine the styles and use whatever you like best or feel most comfortable with. I like using Sympathetic magick when doing long distance healings. I take the candle and see it as the person who is ill, and then I burn away the illness within them. As the candle's illness is removed so is the same healing taking place in the person far away. Oh and always get permission before doing a healing for someone, otherwise it is taking away their choice and that is a violation of the Wiccan Rede.

The other thing is always remember that when ever you are doing any type of magick, but especially this type, you are free to do what ever you will, as long as you do not interfere with someone else's freedom of choice. Also remember in casting magick that the Law of 3 is always there, be it positive or negative it WILL come back to you.

Class #8
Power

© Lady Wolfen Mists Jan.1998

What is magick and how do you use it. Magick is really just the recognition that there are two dual forces in the universe. In the true magickal sense a practitioner has learned to balance and manipulate these forces so that they will better enhance your life and the lives of those around you. Such types of magickal manipulation leads to power. Power is a tempting mistress for many, and as such must be controlled through Humility and Honor. Big words that seem to have lost a lot in this time.

In Wolfen Wicca we put a lot of stock in the bond of giving your word and in words like Humility, Honor and respect. Scott Cunningham wrote of this sentiment in a truly inspiring way. He said the following;

The Law of the Power

By Scott Cunningham

1) The Power shall not be used to bring harm, to injure or control others.

   But if the need rises, the Power shall be used to protect your life or the lives of others.

2) The Power is used only as need dictates.

3) The Power can be used for your own gain, as long as by doing so

   you harm none.

4) It is unwise to accept money for use of the Power, for it can

   quickly control the taker. Be not as those of other religions.

5) Use not the Power for prideful gain, for such cheapens the mysteries

   of Wicca and magic.

6) Ever remember that the Power is the sacred gift of the Goddess and God, and should never be misused or abused.

7) And this is the Law of the Power.

So power must be maintain in balance, as in all things a balance must be struck. All acts in magick, and in life, must ring of balance. You do something for someone and that someone returns to you an equal amount of energy, be it barter for services or gifts or information or cash. It is an agreed upon balance and it must remain so or one feels "ripped off" and this affects the casting of energies and causes the power to be out of balance. As long as the balance is maintained then the power is not in control of the user. It is when the balance is lost that the user looses control and the power takes over. This can happen quickly and ones intent and reasons should always be checked before doing any type of magick.

One test that I always do is ask my self if what I am about to do or request is in the highest interest of not just myself but of the entire universe. If the answer is yes then I go ahead. If the answer is no then I am out of balance and I should reconsider where my intent is. Another quick note should be casting magick when you are hurt or angry. I have a 24-hour rule. I must wait a full 24 hours before I do something to someone who has hurt or offended me. The I ask myself the above question, if what I am about to do or request is in the highest interest of not just myself but of the entire universe. Is it in self-defense? Is this act going to lock our karma together and is it going to come back on me 3 fold or even 10 fold in another life. Jeez if I didn't like them in this life, I really am not going to like them anymore in another life, especially locked into their karmic cycle.

As for self-defense well that depends. Now don't get the idea that I am one of those who picks up the knife and offers you my back again and again. There are times self-defense is needed and the only way out. The question here is how much is self defense and how much is aggressive behavior. In Wolfen Wicca, I expect my students to do the least amount of harm to another that would put them out of the line of fire. In other words no since making the person lose their job and become destitute, when you could easily just get them transfer else where and out of your hair. See the least amount of harm for the biggest effect. However I know that there are times you really would like to see them destitute after all they did to you, it is at these times when you feel so badly that you need to check your balance. What is out of balance that would cause you to feel such

and what do you need to do to bring such energies back into balance.

If you follow these rules you will find as you grown not just in the words of the Goddess and God but in your own spiritual achievements that most of the time it is best to just sit back and let the Lady and Lord take care of it all. Allow the balance to flow through them to you and you will find you are basing your reactions more in loving intent than in the need for power. ☺

Invocation for the Law of 3

© Lady Wolfen Mists 1990

Sweet Mother of the Day & Night
Guide me through this burdensome plight
For all that was sent to me
I now invoke the Law of Three

Send to those who bid me harm
So they may feel their own alarm
Send to those who bid me well
Make their abundance swell

Balance in all that is
It is said the Lady gives
As the mists part the way
The 3 Fold Law was invoked this day

From me to **(name of person)** I do declare
3 times what is owed is fair.
No more do I seek nor do I ask
3 Fold Law will fill the task.

So Mote It Be!

Class #8
Consecration

© Lady Wolfen Mists Aug. 1992

Let's talk about consecration and why we do it. Consecration is of the act of cleaning something, purifying it and re aligning the energies inside of it. In your case we would realign the energies to only do positive work then we would present it to the Lady and Lord. Once they are present we would dedicated it to their service for the rest of our days asking for their blessing upon us, and the tools. The next step would be to present the item to each of the directions (Gates) also repeating the dedication and asking for their blessings for the tool or item.

Why do we consecrate?

We do this for several reasons. The first of which is to remove any negative energies or blockages in an item that may interfere with our use. The second is to make a public statement to the God and Goddess of your intent and your dedication to them. Another reason is so we can empower our items with positive energies so that we can better attune ourselves to their working energies and thus aid us in successful use of our magick. Consecration can act as a 'security" system that helps us to stay on the path we have chosen, keeping in balance all we lean and use (power often needs to be checked and rechecked with our intent, consecration aids in doing this.)

What can we consecrate?

Anything and everything can be consecrated. Consecration aids in balancing all and in keeping our tools cleansed and working. It helps protect them from negative energies and negative attacks that may be focused at them. Consecration also helps the tools store information they gain on the ancient mysteries in such a fashion that they can keep this information safe until you are at a level to access this information an use it without hurting your own spiritual growth. So what can be consecrated, pretty much anything and everything you want to work with on an intimate level and have a successful working relationship with.

Class #8
Consecration Ritual

© Lady Wolfen Mists Aug. 1992

This ritual can be performed at any moon phase. The altar set up is without the pitcher and food plate. The tools to be consecrated should be placed in front of the altar on a small table or such (TV trays work well)

Once the circle has been cast the High Priestess speaks.

High Priestess; "Goddess and God of Light, It is at this time that we gather before you. In honor and reverence we ask that you bless our works that they may ever be in your accord."

Group Response; "Forever on the path with thee"

Now the first participant steps forward to the altar. As the participant moves forward the High Priestadds incense to the charcoal. The participant picks up their tool(s) to be consecrated and holds it in the smoke.

Participant; May this smoke cleanse this **(insert tool name here).** Replacing all negativity with positive. I, **insert your name here**, dedicated this **(insert tool name here)** to the works of the Bright

Lady and Lord. May it be so for as long as I live.

Next the participant walk to the each of the 4 corners (4 gates) and asks the Watchers of the Gates to bless the item also. Say the following at each direction, using the correct direction name.

Participant;   Watcher, great Guardian of **the (East, South, West North**) I present you this tool, **(insert tool name here.)** I have dedicated it to the Lady and Lord. I ask that you bless it also, so that my works may always be positive.

Once this is completed the participant replaces tool on the altar table and the next member moves forward. The new member repeats everything with their tool and this continues till all have consecrated all the tools.

Next the High Priestess speaks, adding more incense to the charcoal;

High Priestess;   "As all have passed through the smoke. The powers of Light have been invoked.

All that's unholy, impure and unclean depart us now, unheard and unseen.

May we and the tools as one self be. Blessed and pure in the service of Thee!

Group Response;	May we walk forever in the path of light.
	May our service be forever in Their sight. "
High Priest/ess; **(together)**	"As we have willed it!"
Group Response;	"So Mote it Be"

This part of the ritual has ended. The circle needs to be banished in a regular fashion. Your tools are now cleansed, blessed, powered up and dedicated to the God and Goddess of Light!

Note to Solitary practitioners:

This ritual was written for group/coven work but can easily be adjusted for a solitary person. All you need do is follow it as written and take on all the parts saying all that is written. If you only have one item to consecrate then you need only present the item to the gates (directions) once asking for blessings and then you can wrap it up. Be sure to banish the circle when you have completed this part of the ritual.

Looking About At a Life Full of Magick

Class #8

Dream Pillow Recipe

© Lady Wolfen Mists Jan.1992

What is a dream Pillow? Its another tool you can easily created to do a specific thing for you. Some people make dream pillows to stop nightmares, others look for love, while still others look for more spiritual gifts. This week's lesson tells to how to make a quick and easy dream pillow. The particular combination given here is to aid you in gaining prophetic dreams.

Please be careful not to ingest these herbs, as some are not considered safe by the FDA for ingestion! So don't eat them and keep them away from the little ones!

Step One

You will need a small pillow cut from cloth (I like cotton it wears well and can be gotten in many colors and designs.) You choose the colors you want your pillow to be. The only thing I suggest is that it be at least 4 x 6 inches. Cut out a template from paper if your not used to sewing, add an 1/2 inch seam all around to allow for stitching the seam. Cut out the 4x6 rectangle and put the cloth so the pretty part (the side you want to see is face to face.) Put this aside for the time being.

Step 2 (need herbs)

The herbs in it are:

Sage for peace, wisdom and healing

Wormwood for psychic powers

Mugwort for prophetic dreams

Mint for refreshment.

Orange peel for focus and clarity

All you need do is hold the items in your hands and visualize that the energies and qualities of each herb becoming one with you. Then draw those energies and qualities to your astral/dreamtime self.

Step 3 (need pillow stuffing)

Now you can hand stitch or machine stitch the rectangle leaving a small opening to turn the bag right side out from and to stuff the pillow from. You will need to stuff the pillow half way then add your herbs. I like putting my herbs in a small lace or net square. I can tie the sides up with a ribbon and it keeps the herbs together inside the pillow. I think they seem to last longer that way.

Then finish stuffing. Stuff as full as you like and finish sewing up the pillow completely.

If you would like you can consecrate this item also when you do your consecration ritual, never hurts to cleanse and consecrate all your tools ☺

Test What you have Learned
Class #8

© Lady Wolfen Mists 2000

True or False

_____ 1. Magick is the recognition that you are the only force in the universe

_____ 2. You can use the power anytime as you wish no matter what.

_____ 3. Poppets are considered contagious magick

_____ 4. Hair is considered contagious magick

Multiple Choice

5. Check the answer Which one of these DOES NOT apply

In consecration we?

(a) ___ Cleanse   (c) _____ Dip the items in day old wine

(b) ___ Realign energies   (d) _____ Remove negative energies

Short Answer

6. Explain the Law of Contact in spell work.

7. Explain the Law of Similarity give examples.

8. Why must we get permission before doing any type of spell casting for another and why is this important?

9. Explain the Law of Three fully

Essay

10. Write a short paragraph on how your **Consecration Ritual** went.

Wolfen Wicca ®
Class #9

© Lady Wolfen Mists Jan.1990

revised 2000

Class #9

Theory;

Psychic Self Defense

Birth Totems

Elements of Magickal Dance

Sacred Chants

All in the Perspective

Healing Ritual

Practical;

No Written Test from this point on

Look up Birth Totem and write a short Paragraph or two in your Grimoire.

Class #9

Psychic Self Defense

Basic Techniques

© Lady Wolfen Mists Jan. 1992

So you think you are being attacked on the psychic level. You have all the symptoms, run down, hurting, everything falling apart at your touch, memories (disturbed sleep) of someone bothering you maybe fighting with you. You are frightened by the thought that someone is attacking you and you give way to fear.

Know that this is a battle and as such the person attacking you has little natural power as they are trying to take yours. This automatically gives you the upper hand and allows you to think calmly. The person posing the attack is insecure and you pose a threat to their image, they have a need to prove themselves the most powerful. This is not what real magick and balance is about so it is bound to be twisted and perverted in nature. So now that you know that you can once more take back the personal balanced power that you have, stop feeding the attacker with your fear and gain the upper hand in your self-defense. Remember that fear give way to control so treat fear as the enemy and move forward through it, the attacker is depending you will fear them. Don't!!! You hold the power of the Universe within you and it is balanced and harmonious there is nothing you ever need fear. The Lady and Lord walk beside you and inside you, you are protected and secure from negative attacks.

However even with this knowledge you may feel a need to defend yourself from the onslaught of things being directed at you. Remember when dealing with the astral realm it works on a different set of principles. There emotions can cause real physical effects on the physical plane and you may want to insure you are protected.

Yet I feel we should take a minute to express the difference between defense and an all out war of destruction. Now just because someone wrongs you doesn't give you open season on that person, karma and the Wiccan Rede still hold you oath bound here. You must decide what the least amount of pain inflicted on this person would be and still produce the desire results of leaving you alone. You cant just wipe them off the face of existence, even thought there

are times it seems this would be the best course of action. The Harm Ye None is still in place (lest in self-defense it be) and the 3-fold law is still lurking about. You must remain balance even in this situation, you must truly wish to end the conflict between you, and return to the balanced serene place you came from before all this started. So a counter attack must be reasonably thought out with mature and thought out actions, not just are action that strikes back. Then once you have accomplished your goal be able to let it go and walk away, no matter how much you would like to "stomp em good" if you bow to this you just set up a karmic cycle that will draw you together again and again.

So with that all said lets move forward to a few techniques that work with much success. The only catch is that you must perform them at least twice a day and in a consistent manner, not hit and miss or when you think of it. If your being attacked then you must defend yourself 24 hours a day, 6 days a week until the conflict has ended. It must be a top priority in your life, so if you aren't dedicated enough to protecting yourself, don't whine about the results to others.

Step # 1

Since your home has bee invaded or is likely to be invaded by the attacking energies of the person and may very well be the focal point for its where you sleep. It must be cleansed and purified! So you must smudge it to begin with any of the incense mentioned below.

Sandalwood   **Sweet Grass**

Nag Champa   **Blue Roses**

Sage

Purification incense made by Lady Wolfen Mists

Protection Incense made by Lady Wolfen Mists

To smudge you need only light the incense and let it smoke in each room and on each wall, allowing the smoke to permeate the room. This removes old misaligned negative energies and set in

positive energies.

Then to seal the energies in Mix the following

>   1 gallon of water (not tap distilled is good)
>
>   1 teaspoon of Orange rind
>
>   1 teaspoon rose water (optional)

Sprinkle the water mixture about the house and say in each room;

Gracious Lady and Lord of Light

Aid me in this attack on me, keep me safe from harm.

Seal my home with only positive energies and allow not negativity to reside with in.

So Mote It Be

That should take care of the house. The next step is cleansing yourself.

STEP #2

Cleansing yourself on both the physical and non physical realms are very important. It aids in dislodging any energies that may have been directed at you during sleep and keeps your armor all tight and clean and protective. The easiest way to do this is to use Armor of Magick bath salts (exclusive of Silver Hoofs Inc.)

To use these draw a bath and put some in the water about 2 tablespoons or more if you want. Continue to fill the bath with as hot a water as you can stand and mix the bath salts into the water in a clock wise manner until they are fully dissolved then get in and soak.

If you are not a bath person like me, you can still use bath salts. Just put them in a small bag (like a muslin bag) and hang them over the shower head. Allow them to mix with the water flowing down over you for a few minutes, imagine you putting on a great impenetrable armor, and then rise with clear water (you may not want bath salts in your hair.) Next get out and dry off, seeing

yourself drying the armor you just put on and you are ready to meet the day. Since this does contain salts you may want to use lotion to counteract the effects of the salts to your skin (it can dry them out.) You will notice right away the armor working as it negates any negative energies sent your way, it has been my experience that this stuff is tremendous.

So that should take care of you and your house, its simple easy to do and fairly effortless on your part.

Step #3

But let's say you have done all that and the attacks still continue. What can you do next? How about trying a simple reflection spell? How do you do it, in your minds eye and on the astral plane see yourself being surrounded by reflective impenetrable glass like substance, allowing only positive energies in reflecting all that is negative and hurtful to you. See it enveloping you in an egg like shape so that all of you is covered by it. Now send your intent/will out to the universe and say;

Negative energies that attack me
Be gone now! Depart and flee!
Nothing that would do me harm
Can enter this reflective charm

Sent back to those that send my way
3 times 3 I send this day
Effect only those who mean me pain
Safe from harm others remain

Now this should work all day long (or as long as you are awake), however when you sleep your shield my fall and then you are open to attack again. So what can you do? Another simple act. Take black obsidian stone and put it close to your bed (sometime inside a pillow case works or under the mattress. Black Obsidian is one of the

few stones that exist on both the astral and physical at the same time in the same place, as such it works back and forth very well. It also will not be in the same presence as negativity and just negates it period. Dissipating it back to the universe in energy form to be used again in a more positive form of creation (in other words it destroys it in the here and now.)

So how's that for simple self-defense? It sounds easy but these techniques are quite effective and have been used with much success. You should with these tools and techniques be able to fend off just about any psychic attack with success. If you need more than you need to speak with a professional in this area and you also need so do some major lifestyle overhaul, for you have been doing something that you shouldn't have to invite such powerful negativity to take shots at you.

Final Thoughts

There is another even simpler way of defending from psychic attacks and that is to inform your God or Goddess, ask them for help and to keep you safe. Follow what they tell you. Be assured that you can rest in the knowledge that they would never cause you harm, for they are unconditional Loving parents and always have your best at heart. Work with them, talk with them and connect with them often and such attacks will never begin in the first place.

Mom Save ME!!!

Class #9

Magickal & Inspired Dance

© Lady Wolfen Mists 1992

In Wicca in general, there is much merriment and revelry. There is also a lot of use of music in ritual and with music comes dance, both sacred and for fun. Sacred Movement (dance) has special elements. With all that said here are the basic elements of magickal dance in Wolfen Wicca®

In all covens there should be magickal dance and there should be a Priest or Priestess of dance that reside over it. It is their duty to pick out the music that is to be used at a particular ritual, along with the High Priestess approval. The dance should reflect the focus of the ritual and the energy needs to be contained and directed. The actual style of the dance can vary from formal (traditional) dance steps to improvised movements. The dancers should be equal in numbers male/female, yet this is not written in stone and no one who wishes to participate should be left out. Any one who wishes to dance should be allowed, as it adds more to the circle and the actual power raised by the ritual.

In the days of old these dances were used to raise the power of the circle to its very peak. Then the pairs (usually female/male) would leave the circle, have sacred sex (often in the form of sex magick, tantra or Kundalini) to increase the effectiveness of the rite. However today that part of the ritual is left out and the rituals power is climaxed with the dancers falling to the floor, all energy from the dance is released to the universe. They are signaled by the priest/ess of the Dance, to end this way prior to the beginning of the dance. This is a signal that the ritual's power has reached its zenith and can now be sent out or released to the universe.

Then the priest/ess places a magickal symbol of the God or Goddess on or before the altar, this has been passed around by the dancers during the dance and helps to keep the balance of energies with in the circle even after the release. Place this symbol on or before the altar helps to insure the success of the rite. If you have never had a chance to see or join in on magickal dance sessions you

should really try, it is intense, tribal and evocative. Words can't express the closeness or the power that builds, even as a solitary practitioner you can enjoy magickal dance, so give it a try! If your not sure what to do or how it should be done take a look at the *elements of dance* out line. It gives general guidelines on Magickal Dance.

Inspired Dance

This type of dance is done without the aid of the priest/ess of the Dance, nothing is pre arranged or thought out it just happens. This type of dancing allows the spirit/astral energy that's created by motivation and movement, to flow out of you. This is a powerful energy that can be harnessed and used by a dancer in a positive helpful way. The dancer must first create a balance between the energy being used and the energy being created. To actually accomplish this is called inspired dance.

It is here that the dancer becomes an "open circuit" to the actual energy, often times losing themselves in the "energy directions" given by the actual dance itself. If this balance isn't struck the dancer can become tired and easily exhausted.

When a group is involved in watching or creating the music the dancer needs to make a positive connection with the group. This allows the dancer to weave the dance with everyone's energies involved and all benefit from the work the dancer does. What the dancer does is use the energy of the group, taking in that energy and converting it to movement and then giving it back to every one in the flowing web weaving steps of the inspired dance.

Sing, Dance, Love Life and Make Your Own
Kinda Magick!

Class #9
Chants

© Lady Wolfen Mists 1992

Chanting works on the same principle of balance as magickal dance, in that it raises energy inside a circle. The energy is then focused and sent out to the universe to accomplish specific goals. Aside from this chanting/singing is fun! It sets the tone in the circle and helps build a specific ambiance. Music/song lifts the Spirit to higher planes of existence and "knowing." Such a gift is a wonderful expression of self. It doesn't matter if it's on key, or if you have the voice of an angel or a frog, it is the expression of the soul and it is meant for everyone to partake in.

Below are some popular chants often used in circles. I have attempted to give credit to the known authors. If I have overlooked someone or mis-credited please forgive me. If I have violated any copyrights please let me know and I will either credit your work on the website (silverhoofs.com) or remove them from further classes whatever the wish of the author.

Fur and Feather

Sable

There are several variations of this one floating about

Fur and Feather and Scale and Skin
Different with out, but the same with in.
Many of body, but one of soul
Through all creatures are the Gods made whole.

The Sacred Space Chant

© Lady Wolfen Mists 12/06/1995

Out of time,
Out of space.
We create
Our Sacred Space

Here we Worship,
Here we play
As we walk
In the lighted way.

Ancient hearts
Call to me
And I enter
In Harmony

Goddess CHANT

Author Unknown to me

I-sis, A-star-te, Di-a-na,
He-ca-te, De-me-ter, Ka-li,
In-na-na.

God Chant

Author Unknown to me

O-din, Cer-nun-nos, Merd-dyn,
Man-na-nan, He-li-os, Shi-va,
Horn-ed One.

Circle Chant for Entering

©Lady Wolfen Mists 1998

Circle Circle
To the Circle I come

Love Love
To the Circle I bring

Trust Trust
With the circle I share

It's the Craft we practice
Its our hearts we bare

To end the chant sing the last verse twice;

It's the Craft we practice
Its our hearts we bare

Beauty Chant

Traditional Tibetan Chant

I like to use this at the end of a circle as coveners file out, very sacred

Oh Go in Beauty,
Peace be with you
Till we meet again in the Light

So go in beauty
Peace be with you
Till we meet again in the Light

Class #9
All in the Perspective

No matter how hard you try at sometime in your journey you are going to have an interaction with someone who condemns your belief system. It can be a Christian or any other faith and it is never "fun" you will feel attacked and maybe even a bit scared, you will want to strike back and "fight" it out with this person. I strongly suggest you don't, never ever get into a "bible" battle with another it's just not worth it.

Instead take a moment and listen to what your intuition is saying. Is this a teaching moment for the person attacking you. Education is nine tenths of the battle and helping them understand us is always worth the time. The following is a personal story that happened to me when a Christian came into my store and wanted to save my soul and tell me I was going to hell.

PERSONAL STORY
****

All In the Perspective- A Christians Question
©by Lady Wolfen Mists June 6 2004 2:34 am

Some one from a main stream Christian religion once asked me if I believed in Miracles and Angels and do I pray when I speak to God? He said he had come to this witch shop to talk to the top witch and that he firmly believed that witches should die because the bible said so, "Suffer ye not a witch to live!"

At that moment I wondered at the wisdom of the Lady and Lord to use me as their vessel in this case. Would I be smart enough or patient enough to answer as my Lady would wish me, would I represent the Wolfen Wicca tradition and the pagan community as they would wish? I took a deep breath and said to the Lady silently. "If you want me to do this I will need your help with speech and

guidance."

Then I took another breath and asked him into my office so we could be comfortable while we talked. He wanted the door left open, I guess he thought my "evil" wouldn't dare touch him with the door open and while he clutched his bible. I not only left the door open I placed his chair in front of it so he would feel more secure about being there and asking his questions. Next I answered his questions calmly and completely.

"Yes I do believe in miracles, those times in life when things are prefect or work out for the highest blessing for all involved. Miracles when so many energies combine as one, with the universe energies, to produce the best most wanted outcome of it all even in a situation even when said situation was the most distressing, no way out times in our lives. Miracles, those times in life when for a few seconds, we reach an understanding of the vast abilities of the Creators. When the plan of the universe seems, for a fleeting second to make sense, when we see the true beauty that abounds about us, and have a deep understanding of it all. Miracles when unconditional love no longer seems a word out there to strive for, but is a real tangible living thing that we can feel and wrap ourselves and others in. **Yes** I do most deeply and ardently believe in miracles.

Angels- without a doubt I believe in Angels, those masters that went before me who guide me and help me make the best journey I can. Spirit Guides who bless me and keep me from harm, entities who are so positive in nature that they make me, in mortal form weep, and wish I too could be as they. Angles who on earth help me, (and others) in the most unexpected times and ways. Angels who work the will of the loving Lady and Lord, and guide me down the Higher Self path so that I may ascend on my spiritual journey. **Yes** I do without a doubt believe in angels, and I often speak and confer with them on many many things.

Pray- **Yes I do pray**. Every time I cast a spell it is a prayer for the aid of the Lady and Lord. Do I pray in humility to the Goddess and God? I do, and even more so when on the astral or within my

circle, when I come into Their presence and spend time with Them. If it be as they feed me cookies and milk healing my hurts or as they teach me their ways down the lighted path or even as they give me my next lesson or job to learn. Yes I do it with love and humility. Do I pray for help when in need to them, yes when in fear I call to my Lord or my Lady I beg for them to lift me up and protect me I ask that they fill me with their white light and keep me from harm. I pray in my daily devotions for this same loving help and direction for all my friends and family. I also pray for the world in general and for those who do not understand, so that their hearts may be open to the Lighted path of my most loving Lady and Lord.

This answer so astounded this Christian, he didn't know what else to say. Soon he stumbled, stuttered and muttered to himself. Then he said "But you're a Witch, you're evil!" I laughed and said "Then so must you be 'cause we both believe in miracles, angels and we both pray to the Creators of life and the universe. We both seek for the Lighted Positive ways and we both wish only the best for those we love, that no harm or hurt or negativity ever befalls them or us if we can help it.

You see it is all perspective that leads the heart. We all walk paths, much the same but different for each individual. Just because the Creators saw to making your path different from mine didn't mean that all such other paths or people are evil. No not at all, it just means that as the Lady and Lord who created all things with great uniqueness and difference, so did they create ways for each of us to reach them, love them and share in the Blessings and Unconditional love they give us all."

This seemed to astound him even more and for the next several months he came to my office at the store asking real questions and sharing insights. Education does wonders to tearing down walls and fears.

I did not change him from Christian to Wiccan (I did not wish to for Christian was where the Universe had best placed him) but I did open his eyes and his heart. At the end of it all he told me he would no longer follow the belief "Suffer ye not a witch to live!" That

he liked and respected me and didn't see any evil in our religion, just another way to God. I cried for his eyes were opened, we could continue to share and the Lady and Lord had used me (this mortal vessel) to work Their will once more! I was glad I had done as They had asked even when I wasn't sure I was up to the task. I was even happier that we had shared questions, answers and made a friendship.

So next time someone questions you, even though you may wonder how in the world could they believe that about you or you wonder if you should waste the time answering. Take a moment and see if this is a time you to can change a perspective, open eyes and teach another about the wonders of being different but alike. Take a second before you lash out at that **stupid question and THINK**, this could be a turning point for this person, you may be being called upon to be an angel on earth to teach and share and build bridges and not make walls. Maybe you too are a vessel the Lady and Lord will use. Try compassion before anger and openness when you can. Who knows this may very well be a lesson for you also.

> May you walk in Her Wisdom and His strength
> Forever In The Loving Service Of Others
> Lady Wolfen Mists

Class #9
Healing Ritual

© Lady Wolfen Mists 1990

This group-healing spell can be easily adjusted for a solitary practitioner. It works best if the person who is to be healed is present, however if this is not possible another 'stand in" can be used or a symbol of the person.

The altar is set in the usual manner, with the exception of a candle set in place of the pitcher for the cakes and wine ritual. This candle is used to symbolize the person being healed and should be colored to suit their zodiac sign, if your not sure of that pick their favorite color. If that's still not possible go with white to symbolize the ill person who requested the healing.

Then a black candle is set on the altar in the place of the plate for cakes. This candle is to symbolize the illness that you will be driving out. Be sure to dress the candle accordingly.

The person who is wishing to be healed sit in the chair, or the item you chose to symbolize them (a picture or such) is placed in the chair all the others circle around. The High Priest/ess then moves forward to light the candle that symbolizes the ill person.

High Priest/ess;

> **"This candle represents, (name), who has come to us for healing.**
>
> **As burns this light in the darkness, so burns the energies within**
>
> **our souls.**
>
> **May our works here tonight purify, and heal (name.)"**

The High Priest/ess now moves toward the black candle. They take some salt from the salt bowl on the altar and encircles the black candle with it. A solid line, making sure there is no breaks in this salt circle. Then the black candle is lit.

High Priest/ess;

> " This candle is to symbolize the pain and despair that has inflicted itself on, (name). We will draw out that pain from (name), and place it in this candle. We heal in the name of the White Lady and Lord.

The High Priest/ess returns to the group. The group now encircles the person once again, making sure to face the ill person. All begin to walk slowly in a deosil fashion around the person. One hand (right hand) raised with the palm up directed at the person. All begin to chant.

Group Chant;

> **"Feel the Power,**
>
> **Feel it Grow**
>
> **Feel the power**
>
> **Make it So!**

While this chant is going on, the group will see themselves covered in white light. This light is directly from the Lady and Lord and is to be directed to the person in need. This will aid you in "seeing" the problem areas. The pace of the chant will pick up as you walk. When the High Priest/ess feels that enough 'White Light" has been directed at the person, they will now change the words of the chant. Lifting both hands at the person, palms up, all members follow.

Group chant;

> **"Heal with power**
> **Heal and grow**
> **Heal with power**
> **Make it So!"**

    The group continues to walk deosil around the person. This time drawing out the negative energies (pain, despair) and holding them with the power of the circle. When the High Priest/ess feels that all have been removed, the High Priest/ess moves to the altar. The rest of the group continues to chant and move around the ill person.

    The High Priest/ess then directs their hands over/around the black candle and pushes the mis aligned negative energies gathered from the ill person. These energies are then contained in the black candle. When the energies have been put into the candle the High Priest/ess moves back to the outside of the circling members with their backs to the chanting members and the next covener moves to the candle and does the same thing.

    When all is finished, all turn (facing) and encircle the person once more. Next they join hands over the ill persons head, directing the White Light once more into the body of the ill person and into themselves. This is an act of cleansing and revitalizing. When the High Priest/ess feels enough has been sent they say;

High Priest/ess;

> **"It is done!**
> **Blessed Be!"**

Then both the black candle and the colored candles are snuffed out, the group says;

Group Response;

"So Mote it Be!
Blessed Be!"

To clean up all you need do is to clean up as usual. Take the Black candle and either bury it or place it in a bag and throw it away. You may give what's left of the colored candle, that symbolized the ill person, to them if you wish. This may be burnt again if they feel it "creeping" back once more.

Wolfen Wicca ®
Class #10

© Lady Wolfen Mists Jan.1990, revised 2000

Theory;

Posted Standards

Key Concepts for Magickal Success

Dark Night Of the Soul

Wolfen: Basics Laws to gauge a coven by & Other sticky Topics

Psychic Gifts definitions

The Cords-Taking your Measure and pushed into circle

Covensteads and Covendoms

Wolf Spirit in your Daily Life

Practical;

Write in your Grimoire about your personal Dark Night of The Soul, if you have had one. What was it like? How did you handle it, how will you handle it. How has Wolfen Wicca prepared you to overcome such dark nights?

Do a Pathwork to find a magickal name.

Class #10

General Laws for the Coven: Posted standards

© Lady Wolfen Mists Jan.1998

The craft is an ancient mystical path. The following set of laws, descriptions and expectations of its members has been developed to be used to govern your grove/coven. These reflect our concerns and important issues. Why have rules at all you ask. We want to be accepted as a religious base and as such we must have some type of laws from which to police our own from. With this set of posted standards you can see if this is the type of group that fits for you and if you fit to the standards of the group.

Duties of the Members;

1. All members will strive to uphold the teachings of the Wiccan Rede! Putting the "Harm Ye None" rule first and foremost in their lives, with the exception of self-defense. For it is from this rule we build our moral and ethical foundation. From this foundation comes our interactions with each other, in perfect love & perfect trust. With this in our hearts we learn to work together as one family, learning growing, nurturing each other and loving. For this is the heart of magick, the great secret of the Cosmos...Harmony in all things and Balance

2. At least once a month all members shall gather, together if possible alone if not, but they shall come to a sacred place and give due worship to the Goddess and God.

Members will be "oath-bound" Meaning that they shall not speak or share or in any way reveal the secrets of the Wolfen Wicca ™. For this is a secret sect and members shall not reveal the workings or any information used in this tradition. It is a vow they make to the God and Goddess and an agreement they enter into with Lady Wolfen Mists. Period!!

3. Members will be expected to give respect, honor and esteem to the High Priestess and High Priest. Remember always they are your clergy, and as such deserve your respect, also remember always that they symbolize the embodiment of the Lady and Lord here on Earth.

4. Members may choose a 1st degree Initiate level for the High Priestess of their grove/coven. Yet, let it be known that <u>only those Initiates of 3rd degree may "break off" and start another coven/grove.</u> This break off must be approved by the ranking 3rd degree, and members may not be taken from the main group if the ranking 3rd degree says no! All covensted Laws must be upheld!

A 2nd degree Initiate can be asked, if the coven/grove gets to large, to lead another group. Yet let it be known that this 2nd degree **MUST** be under the strict supervision of the ranking 3rd degree from the original coven/grove.

5. If there are unresolvable problems/conflicts within the grove, between the Ranking 3rd degree (who is normally the High Priestess) and another 3rd degree Initiate. The other 3rd degree should leave the group. If they choose to create another grove/coven they should not take any members with them nor should they attempt to take over the original group. The reason for this is that it begins WITCH WARS and is a violation of the covenstead laws. It also brings disharmony and negativity to the worship space. Thus breaking the perfect love and perfect trust law. If they are unhappy, if any member is unhappy they are free to move on in their spiritual quest. Yet remember, being Oath-bound is forever.

6. Members will be expected to pay reasonable monthly dues (of cash or barter) to help pay for supplies and such items. No exceptions!

Duties of the Keeper of The Book Of Shadows;

Only one person (the Keeper) besides the High Priestess should write in this book.

1. This book should only be opened by its keeper or the High Priest or High Priestess without special permission

2. There should Only be one copy, as in the days of Old of this book

3. The Book should reside with the High Priestess. If the keeper leaves the coven/grove for some reason, then the duties of this office should be handed to another.

4. If the Keeper should "cross" than that position should be;

    (a) Handed down to Blood Kin, if the kin is old enough, interested or available to do it.

    (b) Held by the High Priestess until another book is made ready, if they choose not to continue in this book

    (c) Given to the Flames, as a show of respect for 30 or more years of service. Saying such a Keeper is irreplaceable. This however is a last resort, for I feel such work should be saved. It is a testament to the keepers work and dedication. I recommend a copy or a page be sacrificed if the coven/grove wishes to make such a statement. Never loose the entire book it is the history of the coven.

Duties of the High Priestess & High Priest;

1. It is the duty of the High Priestess & High Priest to teach, nurture and supervise the Sisters and Brothers in the craft.

2. She or He shall listen to all grievances, complaints & dissatisfaction's with open an understanding ear.

3. They shall temper power with compassion, wisdom with love.

4. She shall always have the right to choose her own High Priest with reflection to the needs of the Grove/Coven. Always balancing Her weakness with His strengths.

5. She shall seek out Elders and High Priest for advice on matters concerning the Grove/Coven. She shall listen to all they say, giving consideration to all.

6. Yet let it be known that **HERS** is the **final word** (judgment), in all matters pertaining to Wicca and the harmony within the coven/grove. She, alone, makes the final decision. Hers is the responsibility and Her word is **LAW!**

Ways of Discipline of Members;

All transgressions against the laws of the grove/coven, shall be punished by the High Priestess. If there is no High Priestess the High Priest shall discipline the member. All members shall understand and accept the ways willingly and by being a member they have consented to this. If they are in conflict with these ways then merry we part.

1. On a full moon, once the circle has been cast grievances that have been presented to the High Priest ahead of time, shall be heard.

2. The accused will take his/her place before the altar, sitting or kneeling.

3. The accuser MUST take the opposite side of the altar, also in a sitting or kneeling position.

4. Charges are read by the High Priest. The High Priestess and High Priest question both sides. Coven/grove members may speak to the High Priestess and High Priest on the issues at hand if they wish.

5. Punishment is decided upon by the High Priestess. However, if she would like to delay, she may do so. The final decision is made by Her, after consulting with the High Priest on His views.

6. If the accused is found innocent that is the end of it. If the accused is found guilty, they are informed of the punishment and the reasons for. High Priestess asks the offender if they feel the punishment is fair and just. They are asked what would be fair in their eyes. She considers and issues a punishment that She considers is fair.

They are then asked if they accept the punishment. If they disagree with the decision, they are then given two choices by the High Priestess.
    (a) Accept the decision with dignity
    (b) Lose their cord of Initiation and possible banishment from the group

Discipline Of The High Priestess & High Priest;

This can only be done when there has been a substantial loss in upholding their duties. Here's the process;

1. The Circle is cast on a full moon

2. A grievance committee is called by one of the members

3. The grievance is aired. Both sides get to talk and explain.

4. All members must be present to vote, secret ballot. If not all members are present then the counting of the ballots is held up until all have been able to cast a vote. The cast ballots are put in a sealed envelope and given to the Keeper of the Book Of Shadows.

5. If found guilty then the High Priestess or High Priest can not be involved in any group practices for a specified period of time (i.e. one full moon usually does it) During this time the High Priest/ess must take time for inner growth work. The High Priest/tess who was not found guilty takes over. If both are found guilty then an alternate is appointed by the grove/coven

6. At the end of the agreed upon time the High Priest/ess returns to full duties, in full capacity.

Class #10
Intent, Visualization & Empowerment
Key Concepts for Magickal Success

© Lady Wolfen Mists Oct. 2000

Intent, Visualization & Empowerment these are all concepts that we think we know and understand but they are much need if you are to move on from beginner level. These are key thoughts that must be clear in your mind, and ones you understand fully, so that you can get the very most out of your magickal abilities.

Intent, we use that word a lot, but what does it really mean to use as practitioners of magick. Intent is where your heart is when you do or ask for something. It is the higher purpose we have in mind for the actions that we take or the gifts that we ask for. Intent needs to be pure and clean, free of ego and of the need for power. It needs to flow from the God and Goddess through us, as their vessel, and out to those it is meant for. Intent is a key fundamental to any spell casting, ritual work or any form of magick you practice. Intent works hand in hand with 3-fold law.

The next idea is visualization, that is the ability to see things, as you want them to be. What the results you are expecting are to be. What you want to see happen with your clear intent. "Seeing" it as it will be, accepting nothing else from the Universe. It is here that your energy is set to task to make your magick work and bring to you that which you have envisioned. This is where focus comes from; you are focusing your intent and visualizing that focused energy into being.

In both intent and in visualization we can use items to help us empower that which we create and authorize in our name and energies. Such items can be stones or incense or even charms or such, just about anything. However these items need to be empowered to aid in a particular way. There are many methods to empower an item this one is simple, straightforward and easy for beginners to use.

Method for Easy Empowerment of an item for a specific reason

1. First I get a clear picture of whatever it is I want. I check my intent and I focus my energies while visualizing what I want for results.

2. I then hold the object to be empowered in my hands or hold my hands over it, allowing the energies to flow out of me to the object.

3. I then call up those who reside at my safe place my animals and my friends and my spirit guides as well as the Lady and Lord and ask for their energies to join mine in the empowerment of this object.

4. I see in my minds eye the joining of energy until it reaches an Electric Blue, and bursts forth from the object. Surrounding the entire object in an egg like (elliptical shape). When this happens I know that the object has taken all the focused energies and intent and visualization it can. It is empowered for the specific reason I created it!

5. I let the energies flow for a few minutes then I sprinkle salt over the object, just a pinch, to set the energies so they don't scatter. I then thank all those that helped create this tool.

6. I set the item in the sunlight for 2 hours as it continues to charge and seal in the energies. Once completely sealed and charged I use the item to draw upon, when I want to focus my intent and my visualization better for the specific reason it was created.

This item I created empowers me to do this in a clearer more concise and direct way. It can be used many times before it is drained of energy. If this happens just redo the empowerment method and its ready to use again. Got that? Ok this might be a bit simpler, say I want to empower a charm

with protective abilities. I do the step by step empowerment method above being sure to empower it with the clear-cut protective qualities I see in my mind's eye. Once that is done I can carry this item and draw upon the energies set inside to empower me with those same protective energies I created in the charm. Make more sense now? Great now go check your intent, visualize what you want and empower something, just to get the feel of it ☺

Class #10

Dark Night of the Soul

© Lady Wolfen Mists Jan. 1998

Here in is an area that I feel must be addressed, it happens way too often and many don't understand it. Many put away their studies and turn from seeking, it is a time we all pass through called **THE DARK NIGHT OF THE SOUL!**

I would like to make it clear I did not write the following but it is a term often spoken of in circles. An affliction, if you will, that hits not just beginners but sometimes the most advanced. I believe that what Fra.: Apfelmann says explains it best.

The Dark Night of the Soul

Fra.: Apfelmann "The Dark Night of the Soul" is the name given to that experience of spiritual desolation that all students of the Occult pass through at one time or another. It is sometimes characterized by feelings that your occult studies or practices are not taken you anywhere, that the initial success that one is sometimes granted after a few months of occult working, has suddenly dried up. There comes a desire to give up on everything, to abandon exercises and meditation, as nothing seems to be working.

St. John of the Cross. a Christian mystic, said of this experience, that it; "...puts the sensory spiritual appetites to sleep, deadens them, and deprives them of the ability to find pleasure in anything. It binds the imagination, and impedes it from doing any good discursive work. It makes the memory cease, the intellect become dark and unable to understand anything, and hence it causes the will to become arid and constrained, and all the faculties empty and useless. And over this hangs a dense and burdensome cloud, which afflicts the soul, and keeps it withdrawn from the good."

Though the beginner may view the onset of such an experience with alarm (I know I did), the "Dark Night" is not something bad or destructive. In one sense it may be seen as a trial, a test by which

the Gods examine our resolve to continue with occult work, and if you are not completely whole-hearted about your magical studies, it is during this period (at its beginning) that you will give up.

The Dark Night of the Soul should be welcomed, once recognized for what it is (I have always received an innate "warning" just before the onset of such a period), as a person might welcome an operation that will secure health and well-being.

St. John of the Cross embraced the souls Dark Night as a Divine Appointment, calling it a period of "sheer grace" and adding; "O guiding Night, O Night more lovely than Dawn, O Night that has united the lover with his beloved Transforming the Lover in her Beloved."

When entering the Dark Night one is overcome by a sense of spiritual dryness and depression. The notion, in some quarters, that all such experiences should be avoided, for a peaceful existence, shows up the superficiality of so much of contemporary living. The Dark Night is a way of bringing the Soul to stillness, so that deep psychic transformation may take place. All distractions must be set aside, and it is no good attempting to fight or channel the bursts of raw energy that from time to time may course through your being. This inner compulsion to set everything aside results in the outer depression, when nothing seems to excite. Last amended June 11, 1989 –

The only thing to do is obey your inner voice and become still, waiting for the inner transformation, (which the "Dark Night" heralds), to take place. You may not be aware for a very long time of the results of that inner change, but when the desire to work comes again and the depression lifts, the Dark Night has (for a moment) passed.

No one can help during this time, and in many cases there is hardly anyone to turn for advice. One must disregard the well-meaning advice of family and friends to "snap out of it" this is no ordinary depression, but a deep spiritual experience which only those who have passed through themselves (in other words to a magical

retreat) but for many, as the routines of everyday life prohibits this, all you can do is cultivate an inner solitude, a stillness and silence of heart, and wait, (like a chrysalis waits for the inner changes that will result in a butterfly) for the Transformation to work itself out.

*There are **many** such "Dark Nights" that the occult seeker must pass through during the mysterious process of mitigation. They are all trials but experience teaches one to cope more efficiently.*
With fractalic greetings and laughter * Fra.: Apfelmann *

So you see if the Dark Night sets itself on you, do not feel alone, for you are one of many. Ride the wave, look deeply into your self, this is a time of close introspection. Allow the transformation to arise. You may wish to speak to others who have passed through it, you may want to rest and re-new in your safe place. Yet know this is normal and that passing through a time of the dark night usually heralds a new level of knowledge and understanding for one, when it has been passed through.

I is Listening and Learning

Class #10
Basic Laws of Wolfen Wicca ® to gage a coven/grove by
&
Other "Sticky" topics; our position on them

© Lady Wolfen Mists Jan.1998

Basic Laws of Wolfen Wicca ® to gauge a coven/grove by

The Craft, being and ancient and honorable religion has a most venerable creed that has been handed down through the ages, mostly in oral tradition and in ideas. If you are seeking a grove/coven places keep these standards in mind. If any coven/grove breaks these standards in any consistent manner, I would suggest you look closely at joining that group.

1. It is the Law of the ancients that all rites and ritual shall be celebrated in secret. That NONE shall reveal the name of the grove/coven, its members or where it meets to anyone. Especially those who are outside the Craft. In other words KEEP SILENT! The reason for this is that in the days of old lives of members depended on silence. Today, we continue this to protect the livelihood of the members from those who do not understand and would do us harm.

2. Harm Ye None! Wiccans, having a deep respect for the Earth Mother and Her Children, do not kill or harm other living things, unless to sustain their own life. This is the basis of the WICCAN REDE and should never be broken. One should never knowingly allow another brother or sister to break this law. Yet a fine line needs to be drawn that you do not set yourself up as the "Wicca police." Balance in all things.

3. There shall **NEVER BE SACRIFICES OF LIFE OR BLOOD**, as this violates the law of ethics and oaths of the Wiccan Rede. Only the Lady and Lord may take that which they create. Sacrifices of the flesh and blood align your soul with the Dark Ones, If you align yourself with these Dark Ones, they will demand more and more from you until your very soul is twisted and sick, as theirs is. Align yourself only with the Bright Lady and Lord, who are pleased with good deeds done in their name.

4. There is no room for ego's or power games in Wolfen Wicca ®; such things will not be tolerated. These are negative traits, which violate the perfect love and perfect trust. All actions should be to honor the Lady and Lord and to increase the harmony of the group.

5. Respect and reverence shall always be expected when working within the circle. It shall also be given to each other and to the High Priestess and High Priest.

6. Responsibility is solely that of the individual member. Do not expect others in your group to be responsible for you. What ever **YOU** put into Wolfen Wicca® is equal and balanced, by what you receive from the craft.

7. Avoid temptation to be malicious and to speak spitefully of the craft in general, of Wolfen Wicca ®, your High Priestess or High Priest or other members, when things do not always go your way.

8. Love is a sacred gift from the Goddess and God. It is never to be entered into in lustful or destroying ways, but only to honor Her. It should life the spirit and soul and not pervert or hinder your spiritual evolution.

9. Laughter is also a gift from the Goddess and God. Seek out laughter in all things and situations in life. Laughter clears the mind and rejuvenates the soul, chases away negativity and cleanses the heart. Remember always that life is to be experienced, enjoyed and above all celebrated. Ours is a religion filled with love and laughter, be pleased with what you are. Honor the Goddess by using your gift to the fullest.

10. To give your word, is a sacred vow. It must be kept no matter what the cost to you. NEVER give your word lightly, stand beside it when you do. For if you lose you honor than what is left for you.

11. Remember that you must hold a high code of ethics. Sure you may slip now and again for we are all learning but you must have a code that you shoot for on a daily basis. Those who partake in our religion must be above reproach, pure in spirit and intent, in mind and soul. They must strive to be honorable, chivalrous, and courageous and have dignity. This is the Old Path and those who walked before us have paved the way, can we offer them anything less? Can we offer anything less to the Lady and Lord or expect less of our selves, for this is the way of Wolfen Wicca ® and the Craft.

Other "Sticky" topics and Wolfen Wicca's ® position on them;
Children

Children are not allowed at rituals or rites. In fact unless the High Priestess (Witch Queen) specifically says children are welcome at something the general rule is they are not. The position here is that it is up to you to provide your child with a religious background and not the coven/grove. When the child reaches the age of maturity they are welcome to join but until then it is requested they not. You must also understand that just because you think your children walk on water it doesn't mean everyone feels that same way. There are

many single people who may like children but prefer to worship without them under foot, just as there are parents who wish to have this sacred time with adults and no children, we must respect this. There are some festivals (usually open to the public) that children are allowed.

Sex

I'm sure everyone has heard about some tradition that makes its students sleep with the High Priest or High Priestess to get their Initiation levels, or some such variation of the story, the One in power calling it the reenactment of the "Great Rite." All I can say to this is **WHAT A LOAD OF CRAP!**

If you are required to participate in such exercises to attain your rank then **run, don't walk, away from these people.** Never should you allow yourself to be violated in such a manner, never would such an ultimatum or prerequisite come for the Bright Lady and Lord. Sex is not something that should be used in such a way and its Morally, Ethically WRONG. No matter how you look at it, it breaks the foundation of the precepts of the Wiccan Rede/ Perfect Trust rules. Such a High Priest or High Priestess is on a power trip, and is not a valid representative of the Lady or Lord.

Such actions have nothing to do with Wicca and everything about being in charge. To me such misuse of power is much like the same abuse of a student teacher and comes down to an almost power rape like scenario. So I guarantee that if anyone ever tells you something like this is a prerequisite to attain a rank in Wolfen Wicca ® they are frauds and not practitioners of the tradition I formed.

There are many more ways to re enact the "Great Rite" like taking the Athame and putting salt on its blade and then putting the blade part down into the Chalice. The symbolism is the same and no one is violated, ethics are maintained and everything runs smoothly. Any High Priestess or High Priest worth their salt knows this and it's just as acceptable, if not more so, than what they are suggesting to you!

Drugs;

I refuse to get into a big debate on this with anyone, the simple fact is they are not necessary to reach a level of communication with the Goddess and God if you have been properly trained, and they are illegal. I in NO WAY will tolerate the use of illegal substances. This means INSIDE the circle and in everyday life. I agree that all people have a right to make choices in their lives, this has never been in question. However "I" as Witch Queen and Founder of Wolfen Wicca ®, have decided NO DRUGS, that is my choice.

In addition to no use of drugs, we will NOT TOLERATE the use of Alcohol prior to a circle function, during a circle function or at any event where circle members congregate as a group. If illegal drugs are discovered the person will be told to leave, no second chances its that simple!

Gays in Wolfen Wicca ®;

We have had many successful gay students in Wolfen Wicca ® as sexual orientation is not really all that important. All that matters is that you find the balance inside yourself. I believe in BALANCE and as such, see the role of the God and Goddess as inter-dependent and necessary to the existence of the other. We do not see these roles as assigned to a specific sex but more to the polarity (energy) of the person. If you are more feminine in nature that's fine, if you are more masculine in nature that's fine also, but just because your soul was assigned to a specific gender doesn't mean your polarity has to be the same as that genders traditional role. Make sense? We are open to fitting to the person not the person fitting to the religion and all are welcome in our tradition.

Questions:

We have spoken a lot about respect and that the High Priestess has the final say, however I don't want this to make you shy of questioning things. I encourage you to pose as many questions as you want. It does not offend me nor does it make me think you are stupid, in fact I think you are searching, thinking and looking deeply. It lets me know you are considering all aspects. Now I may not have the answers to all your questions but I will do my best and if I don't

know I will tell you I don't. We will then search out together an answer and discover something new, learning together is what it's all about. So please ask what ever you need, that's my job and I love it.

<u>Decorum in the Circle;</u>

     Many of you know me personally and some have spoken with me on the phone. I am a person who enjoys laughter and fun (heck my birth name is Joy) I'd be the first to make a joke and to go to a party. Yet with all the laughter and fun there are times that serious things happen in the circle, like Drawing Down, and one needs to be reverent at this time. Just like there are times when laughing is allowed and even encouraged. Remember the Bright Lady and Lord have a wonderful sense of humor and laughter is the most healing salve one can use. So take things seriously that should be taken so, give honor respect to all within the circle and make merry when that time is right for that.

     So that about sums it up I'm sure I have left out tons of info here, but this is just the basic's after all. I could go on about specifics forever. If you have a specific question ask me and I'll do my best to answer it. silverhoofs@att.net

Bright Blessings All,
Lady Wolfen Mists

Class #10

Psychic Gifts

© Lady Wolfen Mists Jan.1998

Many people speak of being Psychic, but what does that really mean. The dictionary states it to basically mean the following;
Psychic: (greek psychiokos - psyche, soul or that which is mental) to sense, to understand and to interpret for practical purposes, a force that enters in and emanates out of the body, mind and/or spiritual or ethereal realms without use of the 5 physical senses .

We all pretty much understand that, psychic is considered paranormal by most but just what are the common psychic gifts one can have. Oh and before you ask, yes everyone is somewhat psychic, in some it just runs closer to the top than others. Also you can have more than one psychic gift so if from the following list you recognize more than one that fits you, its quite possible its true. You know as we grow and learn, gifts are added or enhanced or even remember from past lives so what you have now at the level they are, are not the end all. In the future as you train and grow additional gifts can come your way and you can enhance those you already have.

Clairaudient- (Clear Audio/Hearing)	When one distinguishes and hears sounds or words that seem to be coming from a spiritual./astral planes
Clairempathy- (Clear "emotion")	When one senses or "feels" the temperament, demeanor or emotions of someone else. This feeling is made real and present in the one who is experiencing the Clairempathy
Clairgustance- (Clear tasting")	1. Someone who can taste a substance without putting anything in the mouth, think of a lemon or an orange. See what it does to you mind mouth connection. You can taste it that's an example of Clairgustance. 2. Now take that same idea and put it in the spiritual plane. Here one tastes the essence of a substance through taste however the taste comes from someone or something on the spirit/astral plane.

Clairscent- (Clear Smelling).	One can smell a fragrance, aroma or odor coming from the spirit/astral planes. For example I often smell roses in connection with the Goddess, it is her way of assuring me I am on the right track and that she is at my side.
Clairsentience- (Clear sensation or feeling)	Here one receives or senses information by a 'feeling within the whole body" this information stems from the spirit/astral plane.
Clairtangency- (Clear touching)	More commonly known as Psychometry. One must handle or touch an object/area. Input from that object/area is then made available to the person touching it. It can include such information as the history of the item, anything that may have happened to the owner, who the owner is and on and on. This information can come to the person by any combination of ways, images scents, voices and so on. However this is all information that was not known to the Clairtangent prior to touch/holding the items or area.
Clairvoyant- (Clear vision)	This seems to be the most common one as the media has hooked on to it and made it out in the public eye more than the others are. Here one can actually see into the spirit/astral planes without using physical eyes. They use their 3rd eye and can perceive what is going on there by raising or lowering the vibrational frequency of the 3rd eye and focusing on the energies found there.

Class #10

Cords Color & what they symbolize In Wolfen Wicca®

© Lady Wolfen Mists Jan.1998

If you look at class # 5 under Dressing for Circle you will see that we discussed Robes and the colors different ranking Levels can wear in our Initiatory tradition. Now we will discuss the cords that are worn with the robes, What the colors symbolize and who wears what.

As with tradition the cords must be 9 feet in length, this is considered the best size for a single (solitary circle) and the cord was often said to be used by the solitary to lay out the boundaries of such a circle.

In Wolfen Wicca the males were Red cords and the females wear Green. White is acceptable for both sexes.

Cord Colors	Uses and what the color symbolizes
White	Symbolizes purity, often used for healing and for small children. Also used in Handfastings.
Silver	Usually used as a symbol of the Goddess, Usually in her Moon Aspect. A favorite color of Moon Magick
Gold	Usually used as a symbol of the God. Used to energize in Solar Aspect. This color is often used in Earth magick to symbolize the Earth.
Red	Symbol of the Male energies. Denotes sexuality, fire, passion and activation.
Green	Symbol of Female energies. The Goddess in Summer. Used in fertility magick. Denotes emotion, instinct, and intuition creativity.
Blue	Denotes the Sky Mother and Father. Often used for healing, justice and wisdom.
Purple	Symbolizes Higher spiritual Attainment. Astral Work, Psychic skill and Initiation to the Greater Mysteries. Inner circle color

Class #10

On Being pushed into the Circle & Taking your Measure

© Lady Wolfen Mists March 2000

In the days of Gerald Gardner (founder of the popular Gardnerian tradition) and Alex Sanders (founder of the popular Alexanderian tradition) dedicant's were always pushed into the circle. Many traditions still reflect their influence by saying a truly initiated witch MUST be pushed into the circle.

Such an act was thought to symbolize the students re-birth in the ancient mysteries and from the womb of the Lady. It is said this is the way we are all delivered into the mundane world and like wise it is how we should be delivered in the sacred circle.

As in most Wiccan rite and ritual each tradition has a different way of doing things. This is the way of Wolfen Wicca ® and how we push one into the circle.

1. You are grasp, in front, by the shoulders.

2. Next you are given a kiss on the cheek and told "Behold your birth"

3. Then you are pulled (gently) spinning into the circle in a clock wise (deosil) fashion.

4. You are placed before the Altar and the High Priestess the rest of the rite/ritual continues as scheduled

So if anyone ever doubts your tradition, and if you are a true initiated witch, you can say you were pushed into the circle and re-birthed in to the ancient ways as proudly as any other recognized and

established tradition, and you deserve the same respect as they draw.

Taking your measure

Traditionally this is what is used to take your measure, a purple string and a small black bad to keep it in. What taking your measure consists of is measuring yourself from crown of your head to the soles of your feet with the purple string. Then cutting off what you have measured. Next you take clippings of nails and hair. If you are follicly challenged (a nice word for bald ☺) you can shave your arm hair or just skip this part, and take nail clippings. These are placed in the special bag for just this purpose. You may use any type of bag (muslin or cotton works well) and any color as well as embroidery thread or any type of purple string.

This rite of taking your measure also goes back to the Gardnerian school of thought and the Alexandrian. This was a way that postulant's would openly declare themselves to a coven giving an Oath that they would stay with the coven all the days of their lives. Such measure were given to the High Priestess and kept as a representative of that person.

Gardnerian tradition states that the measure is kept to be used if the person maliciously betrays the circle. The measure is buried with the person so that the betrayer will rot as the measure rots.

Alexanderian tradition states that the measure is given back to the postulant to be worn on their left arm during their 1st degree initiation.

In Wolfen Wicca® it is felt that keeping the measure to do potential harm to another violates the perfect love and perfect trust of the circle. If you don't want to be in the circle in your heart, then by all means do not come. Maybe we don't fit your needs and that's alright, feel free to look for that which does and may we part with a love and merriment between us not dark and nasty energies. In this tradition we do take your measure at your dedication ceremony and give it back to you. It is something you may want to keep yourself, a

memory (magickally charged) of your sacred oath to the Goddess and God, not to me (your High Priestess) or any tradition. Such an oath is sacred between you and the Lady & Lord and should not be minimized by including me (your High Priestess), the coven or the tradition. It may be used later at other levels of Initiation so it is a good thing to keep. You will notice that in Wolfen Wicca ® we choose the color purple for your measurement string. This is because that color reflects A Higher Spirit nature, a connection with the divine self and forces access to Hidden Knowledge and a higher development of psychic abilities. This is a sacred color and seemed most appropriate to such a sacred oath.

Class #10

Covensteads & Covendoms

© Lady Wolfen Mists Jan.1998

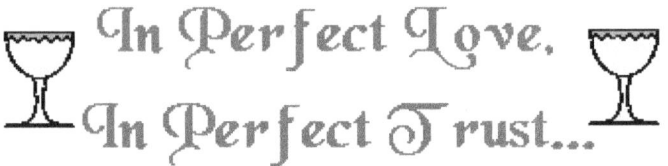

In Perfect Love, In Perfect Trust...

Covens! Words that often strike fear in the hearts of those who don't understand. What is a coven exactly? Well it's a gathering of selected witches that you want to work magick with. It meets regularly (usually on the full moons at least) to worship, play and make magick together together. A coven usually has dedicant's and Initiates involved, and usually has some type of inner circle that one rises to in ranking levels. There is another word that many people hear often and that is grove. Grove is not to be mistaken for the term used by the Druids which is much like our coven but for us means something different. In Wolfen Wicca ® grove denotes a coven that is a teaching coven. One where many beginners (prededicant's and dedicant's) come, and experience the sacred atmosphere. It is usually open to all students and is one where more time is spent on learning the rituals and what one can expect and such.

Covensteads-

Covensteads is the name for the area the coven covers. The actual place (miles) the coven covers. Traditionally covensteads covered and area of **20-60 miles**. In Wolfen Wicca we say a covenstead covers **60 miles.** This means that one coven (of the same tradition or a branch off that tradition meaning a student who has decided to open a new coven) can not come in and set up "shop" in another covensteads area (with in the 60 mile radius in Wolfen Wicca®) without the permission of the High Priestess that already has a coven in that area. Such an act of setting up a new coven without the OK of the High Priestess already there, would violate the Covenstead laws and that coven would not been recognized as valid. This type of behavior, discourteous and disrespectful, is often what starts "witch wars." Such wars are often fierce and not in the best

interest of anyone.

Covendoms-

This is the entire area covered by a coven (tradition) including all the covens and groves that have branched off of the original coven/grove. Covendoms can include other cities, states, and even countries.

Class #10

Wolf Spirit in your Daily Life

© Lady Wolfen Mists Jan. 2001

Each of us holds Wolf Spirit within us, it comes up at different times in our life's and in different forms. Wolf is known to be teacher and parent energy, it drive & guides us, nurtures us to do better here and on the Spiritual Plane. Yet there are various roles or aspects of Wolf that we, as followers of Wolfen Wicca ®, need know recognize and understand how to work with in a successful way. These are not the only Wolves but the more common ones to start off with.

The first form of wolf that we need to be aware of is Second Sight Wolf or Wolf of Highest Intuition. This is the "far seeing" wolf that comes into our lives and aids us. It is the psychic energies in their rawest sense that "gnaws" at your gut. It is here that we learn firsthand, the feeling of protectiveness of being loved by the Goddess, and in showing that love for others. Being in touch with your wolf of second sight allows you to share the loving and protective fore knowledge of intuition! When this wolf pops up in your life... Look, listen and abide by your intuitive thought!

Then there is Sage Wolf, aged and Croned. This is the ancient wolf we all carry inside, who has access to get generations of, stored away and almost lost memories. In this form the wolf within gives us untold wisdom's and knowledge of accomplishments. It can access your ancestors if needed. This Wolf has seen it all, love, death, birth, battles, and more and can share such images and knowledge with you. Sage Wolf should be listened to and honored for they have much to teach us if we listen. When this wolf comes forward to you, you need to look at all the angles of the situation. Gather information and listen to the elders around you for they have much to share to aid you.

The next wolf form within us is the Wolf of Diversion or Silver Wolf. This wolf comes to us when were need to remember that life is to be celebrated and not taken so very seriously that we forget to enjoy it. This wolf self needs to be listened to and played with, as it is as important as any other the other wolf forms. This wolf is friendly, playful. and happy. It plays gently with each of us and teaches us much about ourselves before we even know we have learned anything. This wondrous wolf places us on the road to the achievement of the higher spiritual self, pointing the way in a never-ending game that entices us onward. When this creature comes loping into the scene, you must rest and play and step away from the tediousness of every day life. Take time to enjoy and then look at your priorities. This Wolf loves to show you the importance of connecting with the whole universe and laughing at the beauty and fun things within.

Still another form of Wolf you need to know about is White Wolf. If this great and wondrous animal comes into your life, in physical or dreamtime form, LISTEN and LOOK ABOUT! This is a direct messenger of the Creator/Creatress. It is warning you of something eminent is about to happen. It may also be telling you that you need to look and see if you have strayed from your commitment to the God/Goddess. This is a very serious form and should never be put aside or forgotten. Deep meditation and speaking directly to the God/Goddess will aid you in finding out what this magnificent messenger would have you know.

May You Always Walk In Wisdom,

Lady Wolfen Mists

Class #10

Magickal Name Pathwork

© Lady Wolfen Mists Jan.1998

Do Pathwork (meditation) to find a magickal name

I want you to do pathworking (meditation) for the magickal name there is no real written instructions. By now you have done enough astral work that you can go to your spirit guide on your own, spend time there and speak with your spirit guide. Tell them you need a magical name that will encompass who you are now, one you can share with others. Let them whisper it to you or even spell it out. It may be what you already thought or it maybe something altogether different.

Class #10
Your Dark Night

© Lady Wolfen Mists Jan.1998

Write in your Grimoire about your personal Dark Night of the Soul, if you have had one. What was it like? How did you handle it? How will you handle it in the future? How has Wolfen Wicca® prepared you to overcome such dark nights?

What to do now? Where to go from here?
Step through the Doors

On Becoming Recognized Graduate of this course

which results in

DEDICATION Level

To; My Students
From : Lady Wolfen Mists

    If you are interested in joining this tradition after you finish the classes you can get a hold of me at this e-mail **silverhoofs@att.net** or the website http://www.silverhoofs.com Be sure to mark it Wolfen Wicca 101 Book questions I will do what I can as time allows.

    You will need to send proof that you purchased this book, this can be a receipt or an email from the place you bought it at, like the shipping confirmation to you from Amazon or Lulu. In addition you will need to send copies of the tests as well as copies of your entries into your Grimoire/Book of Shadows when asked to write about an experience to me. To the address you will be given through e-mail. You will also need to write a short typed paper. Don't worry about grammar or spelling or anything like that, as to Why Wolfen Wicca seems to be the tradition you wish to follow and what it has done for you as well as what your expectations of it will be.

    In addition there is an additional fee for the Graduation Certificate and for becoming a member of the Wolfen Wicca Tradition. Be sure to include your Magickal Name and how it is spelled so we can get it right on your graduation certificate and your mailing address you want the package to come to.

    Ok that's it, Hope you had a wonderful experience in reading and learning. I am just an e-mail away and will answer your questions as soon as I can. However there may be time delays as there are many of you and my ol' fingers just don't type so good any more (hee hee)

Blessings,
The Goddess said "Let there be Light" & the God flipped the switch
Lady Wolfen Mists

Other books by Silver Hoofs and Paws Publishing Projects

Coming soon or Already Here

****Angelic Work****

Stop Kickin' my chair

Tools Of Light

****Wicca & Metaphysical topics****

Wolfen Wicca 101

Animal Communication Course
(Part 1 of 3 in shape Shifting Series

****Children's Books****

Knobbly Vol 1

Knobbly Vol 2

www.ingramcontent.com/pod-product-compliance
Lightning Source LLC
Chambersburg PA
CBHW080422230426
43662CB00015B/2183